A GRAMMAR OF THE HITTITE LANGUAGE

LANGUAGES OF THE ANCIENT NEAR EAST

Languages of the Ancient Near East

1. *A Grammar of the Hittite Language*, by Harry A. Hoffner Jr. and H. Craig Melchert
   Part 1: *Reference Grammar*
   Part 2: *Tutorial*
2. *The Akkadian Verb and Its Semitic Background*, by N. J. C. Kouwenberg
3. *Most Probably: Epistemic Modality in Old Babylonian*, by Nathan Wasserman
4. *Conditional Structures in Mesopotamian Old Babylonian*, by Eran Cohen
5. *Mood and Modality in Hurrian*, by Dennis R. M. Campbell
6. *The Verb in the Amarna Letters from Canaan*, by Krzysztof J. Baranowski
7. *Grammar of the Ancient Egyptian Pyramid Texts*, Volume 1: *Unis*, by James P. Allen

8/1. *A Glossary of Old Syrian*, Volume 1: *ʔ–ḳ*, by Joaquín Sanmartín

9. *Middle Egyptian*, by Peter Beylage
10. *Classical Ethiopic: A Grammar of Gəʿəz*, by Josef Tropper and Rebecca Hasselbach-Andee
11. *Ancient Egyptian and Afroasiatic: Rethinking the Origins*, edited by María Victoria Almansa-Villatoro and Silvia Štubňová Nigrelli
12. *Motion, Voice, and Mood in the Semitic Verb*, by Ambjörn Sjörs

Languages of the Ancient Near East: Didactica

1. *Coptic: A Grammar of Its Six Major Dialects*, by James P. Allen

A Grammar of the Hittite Language

Part 2: Tutorial

SECOND EDITION

HARRY A. HOFFNER, JR.† AND H. CRAIG MELCHERT

EISENBRAUNS | University Park, Pennsylvania

Library of Congress Cataloging-in-Publication Data

Names: Hoffner, Harry A., Jr., 1934–2015, author. | Melchert, H. Craig (Harold Craig), 1945– author.
Title: A grammar of the Hittite language / Harry A. Hoffner, Jr. and H. Craig Melchert.
Other titles: Languages of the ancient Near East.
Description: Second edition. | University Park, Pennsylvania : Eisenbrauns, [2024] | Series: Languages of the ancient Near East | Includes bibliographical references and index. | Contents: pt. 1. Reference grammar—pt. 2. Tutorial.
Summary: "A reference grammar of the Hittite language grounded in linguistic and textual analysis, and a tutorial that offers a series of lessons with a comprehensive vocabulary list and illustrative sentences for students to translate"—Provided by publisher.
Identifiers: LCCN 2024016281 | ISBN 9781646022922 (v. 1 ; cloth) | ISBN 9781646022939 (v. 2 ; paperback)
Subjects: LCSH: Hittite language—Grammar.
Classification: LCC P945 .H59 2024 | DDC 491.998—dc23/eng/20240422
LC record available at https://lccn.loc.gov/2024016281

Printed in the United States of America
Published by The Pennsylvania State University Press,
University Park, PA 16802-1003

Eisenbrauns is an imprint of The Pennsylvania State University Press.

The Pennsylvania State University Press is a member of the Association of University Presses.

It is the policy of The Pennsylvania State University Press to use acid-free paper. Publications on uncoated stock satisfy the minimum requirements of American National Standard for Information Sciences—Permanence of Paper for Printed Library Material, ANSI Z39.48–1992.

CONTENTS

Introduction to the Lessons

The following lessons are designed to help you master step-by-step the essentials of Hittite morphology and syntax. Each lesson begins with references to the sections of the grammar where you will find descriptions and illustrations of the grammatical categories being introduced. When you have read this material and memorized the necessary paradigms, you may test your knowledge by working through the translation exercises from Hittite to English. Footnotes give help with special problems or points not yet treated systematically. The vocabulary lists for each lesson give the new words introduced. Words from previous lessons may conveniently be found in the comprehensive vocabulary.

Before beginning lesson 1, you should familiarize yourself with the basics of the Hittite writing system in §§1.1–1.7 and 1.17–1.18 in the grammar and of the phonology in §§1.52–1.54 (vowels) and §§1.103–104 (consonants). Unless you have strong linguistic interests, for purposes of learning the language it is best to learn the details of orthography and phonology as they become relevant in the lessons. It will be helpful to read also §§32.12–32.14 on the conventions for use of superscript in transliterating and transcribing Hittite.

In the vocabularies provided below information is sometimes given as to the grammatical gender of the Hittite word known to underlie Sumerograms or Akkadograms. These notations refer *not* to the grammatical gender of the Sumerian or Akkadian words themselves but rather to the Hittite words for which they stand in Hittite contexts.

Many of the exercise sentences, particularly those in later lessons, are drawn from actual Hittite texts. Those drawn directly from texts, without alteration, are marked with ♦. Those drawn from texts but reproduced here with minor modifications are marked with ◊. The absence of either symbol indicates a sentence was created by the authors.

Lesson 1

Grammar

All Hittite nouns and adjectives are inflected with essentially the same set of endings. For both nouns/adjectives and verbs there are several ways of forming the stems to which the endings are added. This lesson introduces the largest class of nouns and adjectives, those with stems in *-a-*. For an overview, see the table of nominal endings in §3.1, but concentrate on learning how these endings appear with *a*-stem nouns and adjectives by reading §4.1 and memorizing the paradigms for *atta-* 'father' (§4.2), *pēda-* 'place' (§4.6) and *kunna-* 'right-hand' (§4.10). The use of the nominal cases in Hittite resembles that in other case languages: the nominative marks the subject as well as the predicate with "linking verbs" like 'to be', the accusative marks the direct object, the genitive marks possession or appurtenance, the dative-locative marks the indirect object or place where or to which, the ablative marks place from which and the instrumental marks means or accompaniment. The Old Hittite allative marks only place to which. For further details, see chapter 16.

There are two types of Hittite verbs, the so-called *mi-* and *ḫi*-conjugations, whose inflection differs in the singular but not in the plural. This lesson introduces the present indicative of two classes of *mi*-conjugation verbs. Examine just the **present tense** endings of the *mi*-conjugation in the table in §11.6 (avoid being distracted by variants in parentheses and footnotes). This lesson introduces consonantal root stems and stems with the suffix *-nu-*.

I. Some consonantal root stems simply add the endings to an invariant stem. Look at and memorize the **present tense** portion of the paradigm for *karp-* 'to lift' in §12.8. Note in particular the spelling patterns for this and other verbs ending in two consonants.

Other consonantal root stems show an alternation between *e* and *a*. Read §12.2 and learn only the **present tense** portion of the paradigms for *ēpp-* 'seize' and *ēd-* 'to eat' (§12.3), noting the special features of the latter.

Other verbs show an alternation between *e* and zero. Read §12.5 and learn only the **present tense** portion of the paradigm for *kuen-* 'strike; kill' (§12.6).

II. The stem of verbs in *-nu-* does not change. Look at and learn only the **present tense** portion of the paradigm for *waḫnu-* 'to turn (tr.)' (§12.44). But note the special change of the ending *-(nu)weni* to *-(nu)meni* (see §1.133).

Translate the Hittite present tense with an English simple present (e.g., 'goe<u>s</u>'), present progressive ('<u>is</u> go<u>ing</u>'), or future ('<u>will</u> go'), according to what seems most natural for a given sentence. Read §§22.1 and 22.7–22.9 for more on the most common uses of the present tense. Since the verbal endings show person and number of the subject, Hittite, like most such languages, does not use overt personal pronouns for the subject except in cases of emphasis or contrast.

These lessons, with few exceptions, use the most common Hittite word order. Read §§30.1–30.3 for the basic principles of word order. Deviations from the basic order are extremely frequent in actual Hittite, but the conditions for them are best learned gradually. NB that the multiple ambiguity of the ending *-aš* in *a*-stems in particular means that one must pay close attention to the rule of Hittite word order that genitive modifiers **precede** their head noun (exceptions will be avoided in the early lessons).

One important feature of Hittite is that many grammatical morphemes, such as conjunctions, pronouns and "particles," are not independent words but "enclitics" that carry no accent and appear only attached to full words. These are marked in transcription (not in transliteration) with the symbol ⸗.

Since Hittite scribes did not provide punctuation marks, one of the more difficult tasks in learning Hittite is determining the boundaries of clauses. Certain features of word order provide clues. (1) The conjunctions *nu*, *ta* and *šu*, when they are present, always mark the beginning of a clause. (2) The enclitic personal pronouns such as *-mu* 'me', *-tta* 'you' and *-an* 'him, her, it', the quotative *-wa*(*r*), and the reflexive particle *-za* are always attached to **the first word in a clause**, and the local particles such as *-kan*, *-ašta*, *-šan* regularly appear there. (3) If the clause begins with a phrase based upon Akkadian or Sumerian words (*ANA* LUGAL), these particles will be attached to the final word in that short phrase (e.g., *ANA* LUGAL KUR URU*Ḫatti⸗wa⸗kan*). (4) The finite verb normally stands at the end of its clause. In some cases it stands instead at the very beginning for emphasis, but it almost never occurs in the middle of a clause. A combination of features 2, 3 and 4 places the clause boundary in the following sequence of words where marked with #: LÚ.KÚR-*aš⸗za walleškezzi* # *INA* KUR URU*Almina⸗war⸗an⸗kan kattanda ŪL kuwatqa tarnummeni* 'The enemy boasts: "We will not at all allow him down into the land of Almina"'. Beginners have a strong tendency to try to take the words before enclitic elements with the preceding clause; this must be resisted.

Translation Exercise

1.1. *annaš* NINDA-*an* GÍR-*it kuerzi*

1.2. *nu* NINDA-*an atti* ZAG-*it* ŠU-*it*[1] *parā ēpzi*

1.3. *attaš annašš⸗a* NINDA-*an adanzi* GEŠTIN⸗*ya*[2] *akuanzi*

1.4. *attaš⸗za*[3] DUMU.MUNUS⸗*ŠU* ŠU.MEŠ-*it karpzi*

1.5. LÚ.MEŠ-*eš* MUNUS.MEŠ⸗*ya takšan ašanzi*[4]

1. When context makes it clear that a noun phrase belongs to the subject, Hittite may omit any possessive marker. Sentences 1.1–1.3 are meant to go together.

2. Read as GEŠTIN-*ann⸗a*, and see note 219 to §1.148.

3. See §28.26.

4. We intend *ašanzi* here to be a form of *eš-/aš-* 'to reside', as in the Laws §53. Sentences 1.4 and 1.5 illustrate the fact that Sumerograms without phonetic complements are not marked for nominative and accusative. One must use word order and the overall content to determine their syntactic role.

1.6. *mān=mu*[5] NINDA-*an zanuši n=an*[6] *ēdmi*
1.7. LÚ.KÚR-*aš=kan antuḫšuš* GÍR-*it kuenzi*
1.8. NINDA-*an ēzzazzi*[7] GEŠTIN-*an=ma ŪL ekuzzi*
1.9. *attaš* DUMU-*lan* ^GIŠ^GIDRU-*it walḫzi*
1.10. ^LÚ^MUḪALDIM-*aš* ŠAḪ-*an* IZI-*it zanuzzi*
1.11. LÚ.MEŠ-*eš natta ēšteni*[8]
1.12. DUMU.MEŠ É.GAL MUNUS.LUGAL-*aš padān*[9] ^GIŠ^GÌR.GUB *karpanzi*
1.13. LÚ.MEŠ KÚR-*uš=kan*[10] *kiššeruš* GÍR-*az arḫa kuermi*
1.14. GUD (or GU_4)-*aš* ZAG-*an* ^UZU^ZAG.LU-*an* IZI-*it zanumeni n=an*[6] *adueni*
1.15. *mān* NINDA=*YA ēzši MÊ=YA=ya ekušši nu=za* ÌR=*YA ēšši*[11]
1.16. UR.MAḪ-*aš* LÚ-*an naḫšarnuzzi*
1.17. *šumeš* DINGIR.MEŠ-*eš* ḪUR.SAG.MEŠ-*uš* GIŠ.ḪI.A-*it warḫunutteni*
1.18. LÚ KÚR-*i pēran*[12] A.ŠA.ḪI.A-*uš paḫḫašnumeni*

Vocabulary

-a (conj. and focus part.) (geminating preceding consonant)/*-ya* (after vowel) 'and; also' (cf. Latin *-que*)[13]
-a (conj. and focus part.) (non-geminating)/*-ma* (cf. Greek δέ); may mean 'but' (adversative)[14]
anna- (AMA-*(n)a-*) (comm.) 'mother'
antuḫša- (UN-*(š)a-*/LÚ.U_{19}.LU-*a-*) (comm.) 'man, human being'[15]
arḫa 'away, off' (preverb), with some verbs (like *warnu-* 'burn') it denotes completeness ('burn up').
atta- (*ABU/ABI*) (comm.) 'father' (for the Akkadian case endings, see §32.20)
eku-/aku- 'to drink' (see paradigm in §12.3 and note 3 there)
ēpp-/app- 'to take, seize, grasp, hold; *parā ēpp-* 'to hold out (toward someone)'
ēš-/aš- A 'to be'

5. *-mu* is 'for me' (dat.).
6. *-an* is 'it' (acc. sg. comm.), referring back to the common gender noun in the preceding clause.
7. For the special rule that produces the unexpected phonetic sequence expressed by this spelling, see §1.132.
8. The syllabic writing of *natta* (rather than its more common Akkadographic spelling *ŪL/UL*) and the absence of the particle *-za* illustrate features of Old Hittite. See §28.37 and contrast the last clause of sentence 1.15, which shows the New Hittite grammar.
9. This form is Old Hittite (§3.15). A genitive normally precedes the noun on which it depends (§16.51). This genitive marks purpose (§16.40) and is best translated as 'for'.
10. For the construction of LÚ.MEŠ KÚR-*uš kiššeruš*, see §16.19. For the meaning of ablative GÍR-*az*, see §16.90. These two features are specifically New Hittite. For the use of *-kkan*, see §28.101, end.
11. For the use of *-za*, see the refs. in note 8 immediately above.
12. Instead of prepositions Hittite has postpositions, place words that follow the nouns they modify (§20.15). Thus LÚ.KÚR-*i pēran* 'before/in the face of the enemy'.
13. For the uses of the conjunction in this lesson, see §§29.27 and 29.39. The focus particle will be identified when it occurs.
14. For the use of the particle in sentence 1.8, see §28.155, end. Its extremely complex use and difference vs. the conjunction will be introduced as examples warrant.
15. As is clear from the paradigm in §4.2, in older Hittite this noun has a complicated allomorphy, but in NH it is regular *a*-stem *antuḫša-*.

ēš-/aš- B 'to sit, reside' (see §28.29 note 28).
ēd-/ad- 'to eat' (see paradigm in §12.3)
ḫaššuššara- (MUNUS.LUGAL-(*r*)*a-*) (comm.) 'queen' (see for the stem §2.39)
-kkan (see below sub *kuen-*)
karp- 'to lift, raise'
ke/iššara- (ŠU-*(r)a-*, *QATU*) (comm.) 'hand'
kuen-/kun- 'to strike' (without *-kkan*); 'kill' (with *-kkan*) (see §28.114)
kuer-/kur- 'to cut'
kunna- (ZAG-*(n)a-*) 'right-(hand)' (adj.)
mān 'if, whenever' (in Old Hittite also 'when')
naḫšarnu- 'to frighten, terrify, scare'
natta 'not' (usually written as *ŪL* or *UL*)
nu (conj.) (marks beginning of a clause; indicates progression of the action; usually 'and (then)', but sometimes best left untranslated in English) (see §§29.14). *nu* appears as just *n-* before clitics beginning with a vowel (see §1.83)
paḫḫašnu-, *paḫšanu-* 'to protect, guard' (with d.-l. and *pēran* 'against . . .')
paltana- (^{UZU}ZAG.LU-*(n)a-*) (comm.) 'shoulder'
parā 'forth, out' (preverb)
pada- (GÌR-*a-*) (comm.) 'foot'
pēran 'before, in front of' (postposition)
pišena/i- (LÚ-*(n)a/i-*) (comm.) 'man, male person' (in NH, but see §4.73!)
šumeš 'you' (plural)
takšan 'together'
walḫ- (GUL-*aḫḫ-*) 'to strike, hit'
walwa/i- (UR.MAḪ-*a/i-*) (comm.) 'lion'
warḫunu- 'to make rough, bushy'
wiyana- (GEŠTIN-(*n*)*a-*) (comm.) 'wine'
-za (the "reflexive" particle) (its very broad range of uses will be introduced as they occur)
zanu- 'to cook (something)'
A.ŠÀ-*(n)a-* (comm.) 'field'
DINGIR.MEŠ 'gods'
DUMU-*(l)a-* (comm.) 'child; son'
DUMU.É.GAL-*i-* (comm.) 'palace official, courtier' (pl. DUMU.MEŠ É.GAL)
DUMU.MUNUS-*a-* (comm.) 'daughter'
^{GIŠ}GIDRU-*a-* (comm.) 'staff, stick'
GÍR-*a-* (neut.) 'knife'
^{GIŠ}GÌR.GUB 'stool'
GIŠ.ḪI.A 'trees'
GUD (or GU$_4$) 'bovine, cow, steer'
ḪI.A (pl. marker) (used almost exclusively with logograms, and then mostly with those referring to animals or inanimate objects)
ḪUR.SAG-(*r*)*a-* (comm.) 'mountain'
ÌR-*(n)a/i-* (comm.) '(male) servant, (male) slave'
IZI 'fire'
LÚ KÚR-(*n*)*a-* (comm.) 'enemy' (also used as an adj. 'hostile, enemy')

MEŠ (plural marker) (used almost exclusively with logograms (such as ŠU.MEŠ 'hands', MUNUS.MEŠ 'women'); sometimes inserted between components of a complex logogram, such as DUMU.MEŠ É.GAL or LÚ.MEŠ KÚR). See §1.18.

^{LÚ}MUḪALDIM-*a*- (comm.) 'cook'

MUNUS 'woman'

NINDA-*a*- (comm.) 'bread; food' (may stand for more than one Hittite word)

ŠAḪ-*a*- (comm.) 'pig'

MÊ 'water'

-*ŠU* 'his, her, its' (suffixed only to Sumerograms and Akkadian words, not to syllabically written Hittite words)

-*YA* 'my' (suffixed only to Sumerograms and Akkadian words)

Lesson 2

Grammar

This lesson introduces *i*-stem nouns and adjectives. Most nouns in *-i-* add the endings already learned in lesson 1 to a fixed stem in *-i-* (with an inserted glide *-y-* before endings beginning with *-a-*). Read §§4.12 and 4.18 and memorize the paradigms of *ḫalki-* 'grain' (§4.23) and *išpantuzzi-* 'libation' (§4.24). Adjectives in *-i-* regularly show an alternation between a stem in *-i-* and one in *-ay-*. In some cases the *-y-* of the latter is deleted, leading to possible confusion with *a*-stems. Read §§4.34–4.35 and memorize the paradigm of *šalli-* 'large; great' (§4.36). Note the forms with and without *-y-*. A few *i*-stem adjectives show a fixed stem *-i*(*y*)- like the nouns: see the forms of *karuwili-* 'former, primeval' (§4.36, end).

This lesson also introduces the present indicative of *mi*-verbs with stems in *-iya-*. Verbal stems in *-iya-* form one of the largest classes in Hittite. In addition to those verbs that appear exclusively with this stem, there are many more that show a stem in *-iya-* alongside another. Read §12.28 and look over §12.29, memorizing only the **present indicative** portion of the paradigm of *iya-* 'to do, make'. The stem variant with an *-e-* vowel is more common in some persons than others (e.g., third person singular) and much more frequent in the older language than in the later, but one can find either *-iya-* or *-ie-* in any period.

Translation Exercise

2.1. *šallayaš* DINGIR-*LÌ-aš ištanani peran tiyaweni nu ḫaliyaweni*

2.2. *namma šuppin* NINDA-*an* GEŠTIN*=ya mekkin* DINGIR-*LÌ-ni parā appueni n=an=za*[16] *apeniššan iyaweni*

2.3. *mān šallai pedi tiyaši nu* DINGIR.MEŠ-*aš* SÍSKUR.MEŠ *lē karšanuši*

2.4. ^{d}IO DINGIR.MEŠ-*aš ḫantezziš* (*ēšzi*[17]) *ŠUM=ŠU=ya nakkī*

◊ 2.5. IGI-*zian* ^{GIŠ}*ḫurkin* EGIR-*ziš anda*[18] *ŪL wemiyazi*

16. *-an* is 'him' (acc. sg. comm.), referring back to a noun in the preceding clause.

17. See §§22.17 and 30.5.

18. For the position of IGI-*zian* ^{GIŠ}*ḫurkin*, see §§30.27–30.28 (here it is "iconic," reproducing in the word order the reality that the front wheel always comes first). For the position of the preverb *anda*, see

2.6. *mān dankui=ya*[19] *pēdi tiyami nu=mu*[20] *nakkīš* DINGIR-*LÌ-iš ḫuišnuzi nu ŪL ḫarkmi*

2.7. *alpaš maḫḫan ḫarkiš* (*ēšzi*)[17] *nu* TÚG.ḪI.A *ŠA* DINGIR-*LÌ*[21] *QATAMMA ḫargaeš* (*ašanzi*)[17]

2.8. *ḫarkin* NINDA-*an* DINGIR-*LÌ-ni parā appanzi ŪL=ma=an*[16] *ēzzazzi*

2.9. ÌR-*naš ḫuwappaš* (*ešzi*)[17] *nu ḫalkin* A.ŠÀ*kueraz tāyazzi n=an*[16] A.ŠÀ*kueraš* EN-*aš ēpzi*

2.10. LÚ.KÚR-*an šallayaz* URU-*riaz arḫa parḫanzi nu=kan meqqauš*[22] *kunanzi*

2.11. *attaš* DUMU*=ŠU weriyazi n=an*[16] *punušzi*

2.12. *kuwat=wa* DINGIR-*LÌ-aš ḫalkin arḫa warnuši*

2.13. *šuppi* SÍSKUR *karuwiliyaš* DINGIR.MEŠ-*aš iemi*

2.14. *mān* DINGIR.MEŠ-*aš* GIŠZAG.GAR.RA-*az* GEŠTIN-*an tāyatteni nu ḫūdāk ḫarkteni*

2.15. LÚ.KÚR-*aš meqqauš* A.ŠÀ*kueruš arḫa warnuzzi* EGIR-*ezziaz=ma=an*[16] *arḫa parḫueni*

Vocabulary

alpa- (comm.) 'cloud'
anda (see *wemiya-*)
apeniššan (*QATAMMA*) 'thus, so'
appezzi(ya)- (EGIR-*(ez)zi(ya)-*) 'rearmost, last'[23]
appezziyaz (EGIR-*(ezziy)az*) 'afterwards, later'
ḫaliya- 'to bow, prostrate oneself'
ḫalki- (comm.) 'grain; barley'
ḫantezzi(ya)- (IGI-*zi(ya)-*) 'front, foremost, first'[23]
ḫappiriya- (URU-*(ri)ya-*) (comm.) 'city'
ḫark- 'to perish'
ḫarki- 'white'
ḫuišnu- 'to keep alive; rescue, save'
ḫurki- (comm.) 'wheel'
ḫūdāk 'immediately; suddenly'
ḫuwappa- (ḪUL-*(p)a-*) 'bad, evil, malevolent'
išḫā- (EN-*a-*, *BĒLU*) (comm.) 'lord, master; owner'
ištanana- (ZAG.GAR.RA-*(n)a-*) (comm.) 'altar, sacrificial table'
iya- 'to do, make; treat (as)'; (with *-za*) 'to worship'
karšanu- 'to omit, neglect'

§26.3.

19. The *-a/-ya* here is the focus particle, which in this sentence has the meaning 'even'. See §§28.143 and 30.69.

20. *-mu* is 'me' (acc.).

21. On the word order here, see §32.5.

22. As in other languages, the singular of 'enemy' is often used with a collective sense, and subsequent references may use a plural (but see also sentence 15!). See §15.18 on such agreement.

23. This adjective is inflected as an *a*-stem in Old Hittite (stem in *-zziya-*) but as a non-alternating *i*-stem in Middle and New Hittite (stem in *-zzi-*). See note 129 to §4.36 and the paradigm there.

karuwili- 'former, past; primeval'
$^{A.ŠÀ}$*kuera-* (comm.) 'field'
kuwat 'why?'
lē (plus indicative) 'do/shall not' (prohibitive negative) (see §26.15)
maḫḫan (GIM-*an*) 'as, like' (usually in non-initial position; cf. §30.106)
mekki- 'much, many' (often follows its head noun)
nakkī- 'heavy; important; revered, august'[24]
namma (clause-initial) 'then, next'; (non-initial) 'then, again' (see §19.11 with note 65; *ŪL namma* 'no longer' will be introduced in exercise 3)
parḫ- 'to chase'
pēda- (neut.) 'place, spot'
punušš- 'to ask, question, interrogate'
šalli- (GAL-*(l)i-*) 'great, large; adult'
šiun(i)- (DINGIR-*LÌ-n(i)-*) (comm.) 'god' (see §4.45)
šuppi- 'holy, sacred, consecrated'
dankui- (GE_6-*i-*) 'dark, black'
tāye/a- 'to steal' (§12.20)
tiya- 'to step; station oneself'
-wa (*-war-* before vowel) (introduces direct speech) (see §28.2)
warnu- (BIL-*nu-*) 'to burn' (trans.); + preverb *arḫa* 'to burn up, utterly'
wemiya- 'to find'; + preverb *anda* 'to reach, attain, overtake, catch up with'
weriya- 'to call, summon'
SÍSKUR 'sacrifice, ritual'
TÚG-*a-* (comm.) 'cloth, garment'
^{d}10 'Stormgod'
ŠA 'of' (marks following logogram as representing a Hittite genitive)
ŠUM (underlying Hittite word is neut.) 'name'

24. This *i*-stem adjective has a fixed stem like *i*-stem nouns (§4.36). The fixed long vowel of the stem is unique.

Lesson 3

Grammar

This lesson introduces *u*-stem nouns and adjectives. Stems in *-u-* are inflected in a manner completely parallel to those in *-i-*: most nouns show a fixed stem in *-u-* (with insertion of a glide *-w-* before endings beginning with *-a-*). Read §§4.40–4.41 and memorize the paradigms of *ḫaššu-* (LUGAL-*u-*) 'king' (§4.42) and *gēnu-* 'knee' (§4.46). Adjectives show an alternation between a stem in *-u-* and one in *-aw-*. The stem *-aw-* is constant (the *-w-* is never deleted), but note the special form *-amuš* for expected **-awuš* in the accusative plural of the common gender (see §1.134). Read §4.49 and memorize the paradigm of *idālu-* 'bad' (§4.51).

This lesson also introduces the present indicative of *mi*-verbs with the very productive suffixes *-ešš-* and *-āi-*.Verbal stems in *-ešš-* add to a fixed stem the endings already learned in the previous lessons. Study the **present tense** examples in §12.18. Note that these verbs consistently take the present second person singular ending *-ti* instead of *-ši*. Verb stems in *-āi-* are very numerous, and some verbs that originally belong to another class also come to inflect as *āi*-stems. Read §12.35 and memorize only the **present tense** portions of the paradigms of *ḫatrāi-* 'write, send a message' and *ḫandāi-* 'prepare' (§12.36). Note that in the present tense only the third person singular regularly has the stem *-āi-*, while all other forms have *-ā-* (the length of the vowel is not always indicated in the spelling).

Translation Exercise

3.1. ^{NINDA}*ḫaršauš maḫḫan ŠA* LUGAL MUNUS.LUGAL *ḫandānzi nu ŠA* DUMU.MEŠ LUGAL *apeniššan ḫandānzi*[25]

3.2. *idālaweš antuḫšeš* LUGAL-*waš āššū tāyanzi*

3.3. *māḫḫan⸗za* LÚ.KÚR-*aš* URU-*an tarḫueni nu šāru mekki wemiyaweni*

3.4. *mān* ANŠE.KUR.RA.ḪI.A *welluwaz parḫteni n⸗uš*[26] *ŪL namma wemiyatteni*

25. For the order of the head noun and genitive in the first clause, see §16.53. The second genitive here means 'those of the princes'. See §16.46.

26. *-uš* is 'them' (acc. pl. comm.), referring back to the noun in the preceding clause.

3.5. DINGIR.MEŠ EN.MEŠ=*YA*[27] LÚ.MEŠ KÚR É.MEŠ DINGIR-*LÌ=KUNU* *šaruwānzi*

3.6. DINGIR.MEŠ-*aš nemuš*[28] GIŠ-*ruwaš ḫaššuš iyaweni*

3.7. LUGAL-*uš* ^{LÚ}AZU *punušzi* DINGIR-*LÌ-iš=wa kuwat kartimmiešzi*

♦ 3.8. *nu ANA ABU=YA* MUNUS.LUGAL <(KUR)> ^{URU}*Mizri*[29] *tuppiyaz* EGIR-*pa kiššan ḫatraizzi kuwat=wa apeniššan TAQBI*[30]

3.9. LUGAL-*waš* DUMU.MEŠ-*eš makkeššanzi šalleššanzi=ya*

3.10. DUMU.É.GAL *genuwaš* GAD-*an*[31] LUGAL-*ui parā ēpzi*

3.11. LUGAL-*waš tueggaz idālu arḫa parḫmi*

3.12. *daššuš* DINGIR-*LÌ-iš* ḪUR.SAG-*an pedi=šši*[32] *katta tarmāizzi*

3.13. ^{LÚ}SANGA-*iš pargawaz* ḪUR.SAG.MEŠ-*az ḫalluwaz ḫariyaz* DINGIR.MEŠ-*uš weriyazzi*

3.14. *mān=za parkuiš ēšmi nu=mu*[33] DINGIR.MEŠ-*eš ganeššanzi nu daššešmi*[34]

3.15. DINGIR.MEŠ-*eš parkuin antuḫšan šarlānzi daššanuwanzi=ya=an*[35]

Vocabulary

āppa (EGIR-*pa*) 'back; again'

āššu- 'good'; as neuter collective noun 'goods' (see §3.24, end, for the spelling *āššū* and its idiomatic sense)

ḫallu- 'deep'

ḫandāi- 'to align; arrange, prepare'

ḫāriya- (comm.) 'valley'

^{NINDA}*ḫarši-* (NINDA.GUR$_4$.RA-*i-*) (comm.) 'leavened bread'[36]

ḫāšša- (GUNNI-*a-*) (comm.) 'hearth'

ḫaššu- (LUGAL-*u-*) (comm.) 'king'

ḫatrāi- 'to send a message (about), write (about)'

idālu- (ḪUL-(*l*)*u-*) 'bad, evil; hostile'

ganešš- 'to recognize, acknowledge'

kartimmiešš- 'to become angry'

katta (GAM) 'down(ward)'

27. This phrase is a vocative. See §§16.9–16.10.

28. *nemuš* is the regular accusative plural common gender of *newa-*. See §1.134.

29. KUR added here from the duplicate. We write *Mizri* in capitalized lower case, like a Hittite word, but in KUR ^{URU}x the word written 'x' is a stem form used like a logogram (cf. §1.51)—some use all upper case (*MIZRI*). MUNUS.LUGAL KUR ^{URU}*Mizri* stands for **Mizriyaš utne(y)aš ḫaššuššaraš* 'queen of the land of Egypt' in Hittite, with *Mizriyaš utneyaš* 'of the land of Egypt' as genitives dependent upon the nominative *ḫaššuššaraš* 'queen'. Cf. §32.5.

30. *TAQBI* is Akkadian 'you spoke' (pret. 2 sg.); see §§32.29 and 32.35.

31. This is the standard Hittite expression for a napkin used to protect the royal couple's consecrated garments during bouts of libating and breaking bread offerings.

32. The *-šši* is possessive 'its'.

33. *-mu* is 'me' (acc.).

34. While *nu* may be rendered simply 'and', this is an example where 'so (that)' would also be apt (cf.§30.50).

35. *-an* is 'him' (acc. sg. comm.), referring back to the noun in the preceding clause.

36. This *i*-stem noun shows an alternating stem *ḫarši-/ḫarša(y)-* (see §4.28).

gēnu- (neut.) 'knee'
kiššan 'thus, as follows'
makkešš- 'to multiply (intr.), become numerous'
(URU)*Mizra/i-* 'Egypt'[37]
nēwa- (GIBIL) 'new'
parku- 'high'
parkui- 'pure'
šallešš- 'to grow large; grow up'
LÚ*šankunni-* (LÚSANGA-*(n)i-*) (comm.) 'priest'
šarlāi- 'to exalt, praise'
šāru- (neut.) 'booty, plunder'
šaruwāi- 'to plunder' (for older *šāruwe/a-*; cf. §§12.20 and 12.49)
tarḫu-/taruḫ- (+ *-za*) 'to conquer', (without *-za*) 'to be superior' (for the inflection, see §12.12; for the transitivizing force of *-za* §28.31)
tarmāi- 'to nail, fasten'
tāru- (GIŠ-*(r)u-*) (neut.) 'wood; tree'
daš(ša)nu- 'to make powerful'
daššešš- 'to become powerful'
daššu- 'mighty, powerful'
tuegga- (NÍ.TE) (comm.) 'body, limb'
tuppi- (neut.) (Sum. DUB; Akkad. *ṬUPPU*) 'clay tablet'
wellu- (Ú.SAL-*u-*) (comm.) 'meadow, pasture'
ANŠE.KUR.RA-*u-* (comm.) 'horse'
LÚAZU (comm.) ' exorcist'
DUMU LUGAL-*a-* (comm.) 'prince'
É DINGIR-*LÌ* (neut.) 'temple'
GAD-*a-* (comm.) '(piece of) cloth'
KUR (neut.) 'land, country'
ANA 'to, for' (marks a following uninflected word as dative-locative case)
-KUNU 'your' (plural) (used only after Sumerograms and Akkadian words)

37. Since most lands familiar to the Hittites were or began as city-states, including empires like Assur and eventually their own, Hittite scribes sometimes also added URU as a determinative even for Egypt.

Lesson 4

Grammar

This lesson introduces the common verbs 'to go' and 'to come', infinitives, and enclitic pronouns. Memorize only the **present tense** portion of the paradigms for *pa(i)-* 'go' and *uwa-* 'come' (§12.41). Besides functioning as ordinary motion verbs, *pa(i)-* and *uwa-* are also used in a serial construction with another finite verb. For the meaning of this construction in the present tense, read for now §§24.30 and 24.35. Complications will be treated in footnotes as needed.

Hittite has a single infinitive formed with one of the two suffixes *-anna* and *-wanzi*. Read §11.30 for a description of which suffix occurs with a given verbal stem (NB also in §11.28 that verbs with stem alternation regularly form the infinitive from the same stem as the present third person plural). For reading texts it is unnecessary to memorize the suffix for every individual verb. What is important is to recognize verbal forms in *-anna* and *-wanzi* as infinitives. Read §§25.9 and 25.16 for the most common uses of the infinitive (others may be ignored for now). Pay special attention to the unexpected use of the **dative-locative** for the direct object of an infinitive (§25.14) alongside the expected **accusative** (§§25.12–25.13).

The widespread use in Hittite of "enclitics" (many of which are attached to the first full word in a clause or to the conjunction *nu*) has already been briefly described in the introduction to lesson 1. Read now §30.18 to familiarize yourself with the **basics** of how this system works, with special attention to the fixed **order** in which various enclitics occur. The usage of many enclitic particles is too complex to be presented in full in these lessons (for full discussion, see chapter 28). Footnotes will convey their meaning as they occur in individual sentences.

In order to create plausible Hittite multi-clause sentences, we have already used several examples of one important class: **enclitic personal pronouns**. It is now time to learn them in full (you will notice at once how many more sentences based on real Hittite are now possible). Memorize the forms in §5.10 and note the rules governing their order in §30.21. The vowel of the conjunction *nu* is deleted before those beginning with a vowel: *nu+aš* > *n=aš*, etc. (§1.83). The principal use of Hittite enclitic personal pronouns is, as with English pronouns, to refer to participants in the discourse (speaker and hearer) or other referents mentioned in the discourse. The reference is almost always to those previously mentioned ("anaphoric"). Forward reference ("cataphoric") is rare. Hittite has accented pronouns for all three persons, which are only used for emphasis or contrast (treated in lessons 10 and 11). There are no enclitic subject pronouns for the first and second persons ('I, we, you'), and third person enclitic subject pronouns are not needed with most verbs. Some **intransitive** verbs—a few of which occur very frequently ('go', 'come', etc.)—require enclitic pronominal subjects. Read §§17.15–17.16 for a description. It is **not** necessary at this point to memorize all the details of this distribution. What is important to remember is that **transitive** verbs never take enclitic subject pronouns. This fact can help greatly in disambiguating the meaning of *-e*, *-aš* and *-at*. If one of these pronouns occurs in the same clause as a **transitive** verb, it must represent the **direct object**. Conversely, if it co-occurs with an **intransitive** verb, it must be the **subject**. Keep this in mind in translating the sentences in this and the following lessons.

Hittite regularly uses enclitic pronouns to mark direct and indirect objects. Note that for the first and second person the same form is used for both direct and indirect objects—which one is intended must be determined from the context. The third person pronouns share some endings with the nouns (*-aš*, *-an*), but others are peculiar to the pronouns (*-at*, *-e*). A special difficulty is presented by the fact that several of these are ambiguous in meaning: note carefully the two meanings of Old Hittite *-e* and of New Hittite (henceforth NH) *-aš* and the **three** meanings of NH *-at* (see again §5.10).

Translation Exercise

4.1. *mān⸗za* LUGAL-*uš* MUNUS.LUGAL-*ašš⸗a* DINGIR.MEŠ-*muš*[38] *iyanzi n⸗aš* DINGIR.MEŠ-*eš luluwanzi*

4.2. *maḫḫan⸗kan* ^{d}UTU-*uš šallayaz arunaz šarā uezzi nu⸗šši⸗kan*[39] *menaḫḫanda tiyaweni*

4.3. LUGAL.GAL *INA* KUR LÚ.KÚR *paizzi nu mekkauš* URU.ḪI.A-*uš wal(a)ḫzi*

♦ 4.4. $^{\text{LÚ.MEŠ}}$*ḫallirieš* SÌR-*RU* $^{\text{LÚ.MEŠ}}$*zinḫūrieš tarkuanzi t⸗e⸗šta pānzi*[40]

4.5. *maḫḫan* LÚ.KÚR-*an arḫa parḫueni n⸗aš aruna paizzi*

4.6. *mān⸗kan*[41] *šarkun* DINGIR-*LA*$_{12}$ ^{NINDA}*ḫaršit aššanumeni nu⸗nnaš*[42]*⸗aš genzuwalaš*

◊ 4.7. *mān(⸗za)* 1-*EN* URU-*LU*$_{4}$*⸗ya ēpti*[43] *nu kāšma NIŠ* DINGIR-*LÌ ŪL paḫḫašnuši n⸗an*[44] *uwammi* LÚ.KÚR-*aš iwar* GUL-*aḫmi*

4.8. *nu⸗šmaš⸗kan* EN⸗*ŠUNU kuit* BA.ÚŠ[45] *nu* LÚ.MEŠ KUR ^{URU}*Mizri naḫšariyanzi*[46]

38. For the shape of acc. pl. DINGIR.MEŠ-*muš* (*šimuš*), see §§1.134 and 4.45.

39. *-kkan* is obligatory with *menaḫḫanda tiya-* and a dative: see CHD L-N 275b 1 a 3′.

40. For the conjunction *ta*, see §§29.10–29.11 and for the particle *-(a)šta* §§28.65 and 28.69.

41. A local particle (one in the class of *-kkan*) is obligatory with the verb *aš(ša)nu-*.

42. *-(n)naš* is dative here.

43. In this NH sentence the *mi*-verb *ēpp-* ending in a consonant regularly takes pres. 2 sg. *-tti* (cf. §11.11).

44. The context makes clear that *-an* (acc. sg. comm.) refers back to the 1-*EN* URU-*LU*$_{4}$, not the oath.

45. The particle *-kkan* underscores here that the action of the verb affects those referred to by *-šmaš* (see §28.113).

46. The context shows that *naḫšariyanzi* refers to a past action. For this use of the present tense, see §22.14. In the real Hittite sentence on which this invented example is modeled (see sentence 6.2 in lesson 6!) the function is foregrounding.

◊ 4.9. [*našm*]*a*[47]*=šmaš DINU=ma kuitki*[48] *nu lē nuntarnutteni* . . . [*nu=kan*[49]] *lē idālawēštēni*

4.10. *nu=kan*[50] LUGAL-*uš šuḫḫi šarā paizzi n=aš ANA* ^{d}UTU *ŠAMÊ UŠKEN*

4.11. [51]*kuwat uwaši* [51]DINGIR.MEŠ-*aš* ^{UZU}*šuppaš ḫandawanzi uwami*

♦4.12. *nu=kan* ^{URU}*Piqainarišaz arḫa* ^{URU}*Aštigurqa anda paizzi*[52]

4.13. *maḫḫan=ašta*[53] MUNUS.LUGAL-*aš IŠTU* É.GAL-*LÌ parā uezzi nu* DUMU.MEŠ É.GAL *kunnaz* GÙB-*lazzi=ya*[54] *tiyanzi*

4.14. *mān* LÚ.KÚR-*aš ANA* ZAG.ḪI.A KUR ^{URU}*Ḫatti* GUL-*aḫḫuwanzi uezzi* KUR*=KA=aš=kan*[55] *ištarna arḫa lē paizzi*

4.15. *mān* LUGAL-*i āššu*[56] *n=aš adanna akuwanna paizzi*

Vocabulary

anda (preverb) 'in(to)'
aruna- (A.AB.BA) (comm.) 'sea'
aš(ša)nu- 'to make right; arrange'
^{LÚ}*ḫalliri-* (comm.) (a cult functionary)
irḫa- (ZAG-*a-*) (comm.) 'border; border territory'
^{d}*Ištanu-* (^{d}UTU-*u-*) (comm.) 'sun; Sun-god'
ištarna arḫa 'through, across' (takes the accusative)
idālawešš- 'to become bad/inimical'
iwar 'as, like' (with preceding genitive) (§§16.44–16.45)
kāša and *kāšatta/kāšma* 'look (here)', 'look (there)' (on the force of these words, often best freely translated or left untranslated, see §§17.45–17.48)
genzuwala- 'merciful'
kuit 'because, since' (only from MH; never clause-initial; cf. §§30.62–30.65)
luluwāi- 'to make prosper'
maḫḫan (GIM-*an*) 'when, as soon as' (in clause-initial position; cf. §30.57)
menaḫḫanda (IGI-*anda*) 'towards, facing' (with dat.-loc.)

47. *našma* should be translated as 'or if' here, as the first clause is a conditional one.

48. *kuitki* is 'some' (nom.-acc. sg. neut.) modifying *DINU*. For the syntax, see §16.58. We will no longer footnote the regular and grammatical omission of finite 'to be' in the present tense.

49. See §28.112 on the use of *-kkan*.

50. See §28.107.

51. Asyndeton is regular in the first clause of direct quotes. In a dialogue the first clause of each successive speaker will be asyndetic. See §29.47.

52. This example taken from an oracular inquiry about which route the Hittite king should follow may be taken as a question or a statement (in the latter case as a proposal) to be approved or rejected by the oracle procedure: 'shall he' or 'he will'. The absence of a subject clitic pronoun with *pai-* is conditioned as per §17.21. The position of the preverb *arḫa* suggests that both it and the preceding ablative have been topicalized (cf. §30.27, end). This means that *arḫa* cannot be proven to be a postposition here, but it cannot be entirely excluded (cf. §§20.38–20.40).

53. See §28.65.

54. For the ending of GÙB-*lazzi*, see §1.148 note 220.

55. See §28.111.

56. This clause illustrates a common expression for 'if it please(s) . . . (plus dative)'. Note the lack of an enclitic subject pronoun for non-referential 'it'. Such clauses can also have a real subject: *namma=šši mān* ^{DUG}*ḫaršiyalli aššu* 'Then if he wishes *ḫaršiyalli*-vessels, . . .' KUB 7.5 iv 12–13.

naḫšariya- ‘to be(come) afraid’
našma ‘or’
nuntarnu- ‘to hasten, act hastily’
pai- ‘to go’ (with preverbs indicating direction)
šarā ‘up, upward’
šarku- ‘exalted’
šuḫḫa- (comm.) ‘roof’
^{UZU}*šuppa-* ‘sacralized/consecrated meat’ (collective plural only)[57]
tarku-/taruk- ‘to dance’ (§12.12)
uwa-, *ue-* ‘to come’
^{LÚ} *zinḫuri-* (comm.) (a cult functionary)
BA.ÚŠ ‘died’ (§32.7)
É.GAL-*LÌ* ‘palace’
GÙB-*(l)a-* ‘left-(hand)’ (adj.)
SÌR-*RU* ‘they sing’ (= *IZAMMARŪ*, see §§32.29 and 32.33)
^{d}UTU-*ŠI* ‘my Sungod’ (royal title; usually translated ‘His Majesty’)[58]
1-*EN* ‘one’ (the complement -*EN* represents the end of the Akkadian word *išten* ‘one’)
DĪNU ‘legal case, dispute’
INA ‘in, into’ (marks dative-locative case)
IŠTU (marks ablative or instrumental case, thus ‘from’ or ‘with’)
-*KA* ‘your’ (sg.) (used only after Sumerograms and Akkadian words)
NĪŠ DINGIR-*LÌ* ‘oath’
ŠAMÊ ‘of heaven’
-*ŠUNU* ‘their’ (used only after Sumerograms and Akkadian words)
UŠKÊN ‘bows’

57. This noun is the lexicalized original collective nom.-acc. plural of the adjective *šuppi-*. See §4.7.

58. This royal title, indicating an identification of the king with the Sungod, the god of justice, whose typical dress he at times shared, is also indicated on the royal seal by the use of the winged sun-disk over the royal name. The Hittite king was not, however, considered divine while he was alive. Cf. §32.25 note 9.

Lesson 5

Grammar

This lesson introduces common gender nouns in *-tt-*, nouns and adjectives in *-nt-* and the present indicative of verbs with an infix *-ni(n)-*. For nouns in *-tt-*, read §§4.92–4.94 and memorize the paradigms of *wē/ītt-* 'year', *kāšt-* 'hunger, famine' and *aniyatt-* 'ritual' (§4.95). For adjectives in *-nt-*, read §§4.98–4.99 and memorize the paradigm of *ḫūmant-* 'all'. Nouns in *-nt-* (all common gender—see §4.98) are inflected just like the adjectives (see the paradigm of *išpant-* 'night' in §4.99).

Hittite has a single participle, formed with a suffix *-ant-* and inflected just like other adjectives in *-nt-*. It is built to the regular verbal stem, the same stem as the present third person plural in those cases where there is stem variation (e.g., *appant-* 'seized', *kurant-* 'cut', *ḫandānt-* 'prepared, arranged'). Read §§25.36–25.42 for the meaning and usage of the participles. Note that with rare exceptions (§25.36), participles have a passive meaning when formed from transitive verbs. Sometimes they form an "analytic perfect" tense with the verbs *ḫar(k)-* 'to have' or *ēš-* 'to be': read carefully §22.18 on how these constructions are used, focusing for now only on the construction with *ēš-* (§§22.22-22.23)[59] and remembering that the verb 'to be' is sometimes left unexpressed (§22.17).

A small class of verbs ending in a *-k-* form their stem by **inserting** an "infix" *-ni(n)-* before the final *-k-*. Memorize the **present tense** portion of the paradigm of *ḫarnink-* 'destroy' (§12.16), noting the distribution of the variants *-nik-* and *-nink-*.

Note on Transliteration. In the first four lessons the translation exercises have been presented in so-called bound transcription, with the morpheme boundaries before enclitics marked with (=). But published editions of Hittite texts use transliteration, for it more directly reflects how the texts are written in the cuneiform originals. Therefore, beginning in lesson 5 the exercises are given in transliteration. To aid students make the transition from bound transcription, in lessons 5–9 transliterated Hittite texts are followed by the same selections in bound transcription. The latter should help in interpreting the former. Beginning with lesson 10, **only** transliteration will be used.

59. For the *ḫar(k)-* construction, see lesson 6.

Translation Exercise

5.1. LUGAL-*uš* LÚ.KÚR-*an* UD.KAM-*az*[60] *wa-al-aḫ-zi iš-pa-an-ta-az-ma-aš*[60] *tu-uz-zi-ya-zi*

5.2. *ú-e-ri-ya-an-te-eš Ú-UL-ya ú-e-ri-ya-an-te-eš* DINGIR.MEŠ-*eš A-NA* SÍSKUR *ú-wa-an-zi*

5.3. DINGIR.MEŠ-*aš ú-e-ri-ya-wa-an-zi pa-i-u-e-ni ḫa-an-te-ez-zi-ma-at* UD-*ti Ú-UL ú-wa-an-zi*

5.4. $^{\text{LÚ.MEŠ}}$SANGA-*eš* DINGIR.MEŠ-*uš pu-nu-uš-ša-an-zi kar-tim-mi-ya-at-ti-wa pé-e-ra-an*[61] *Ú-UL ú-wa-at-te-ni*

5.5. MU.KAM-*za ku-it* LUGAL-*wa-aš* ÉRIN.MEŠ-*ti še-er te-pa-u-eš-ša-an-za*[62] *na-at a-ap-pa* ^{URU}*Ḫa-at-tu-ša pa-a-an-zi*

◊ 5.6. *iš-pa-an-ti-iš-ša-an ša-aš-ti*[63] *ša-ne-ez-zi-iš te-eš-ḫa-aš an-tu-uḫ-ša-an pí-it-tu-li-ya-an-ta-an*[64] *na-at-ta e-ep-zi*

♦ 5.7. *ták-ku* LÚ.U$_{19}$.LU-*an ku-iš-ki*[65] *ḫu-ú-ni-ik-zi ta-an iš-tar-ni-ik-zi nu a-pu-u-un*[66] *ša-a-ak-ta-a-iz-zi*

5.8. *ma-a-aḫ-ḫa-an ki-iš-ša-an iš-ta-ma-aš-mi* ^{LÚ}KÚR-*aš-wa ú-ez-zi nu-za* ÉRIN.MEŠ ANŠE.KUR.RA.MEŠ-*ya ni-ni-ik-mi*

◊ 5.9. *nu-za* LUGAL-*uš* ^{URU}*Tu-wa-nu-wa-an za-aḫ-ḫi-ya-u-wa-an-zi e-ep-zi*[67]

5.10. *an-tu-uḫ-še-eš ḫu-u-ma-an-te-eš da-lu-ga-uš* MU.KAM.ḪI.A-*uš du-uš-ga-ra-at-ta-an-na ša-an-ḫa-an-zi*

5.11. EN-*aš me-ek-ki kar-tim-mi-ya-wa-an-za nu na-aḫ-ša-ra-az* ÌR.MEŠ-*uš e-ep-zi*

5.12. LUGAL-*uš-za ŠA* LÚ.KÚR ÉRIN.MEŠ-*an tar-uḫ-zi nu ku-na-an-za-aš-ša*[68] *me-ek-ki*[69] ^{LÚ}*ap-pa-an-za-aš-ša*[68] *me-ek-ki*[69]

◊5.13. *nu-ut-ta*[70] *ka-a-aš-ma tar-pa-aš-ša-an ú-nu-wa-an-da-an pí-ya-mi na-aš-kán*[71] *ḫu-u-ma-an-da-az*[72] *aš-ša-nu-wa-an-za*

60. The ablatives of 'day' and 'night' mean 'by day' and 'at/by night'.

61. On this use of *pēran*, see §20.29, end.

62. The context suggests that the verb expresses an event (winter is coming), not a state, so this is an analytic perfect. One should supply 'too', a degree adverb for which Hittite has no equivalent.

63. Both dat.-loc. nominals expressing time and place have been topicalized (cf. §30.27, end).

64. For this participle as "depictive" ('in an anxious state'), describing a circumstance, not an inherent quality, see §25.39, following Rieken.

65. *kuiški* is 'someone, anyone' (nom. sg. comm.).

66. *apūn* is 'him, that one' (acc. sg. comm.), referring to the injured party.

67. For the meaning of *-za* plus *ēpp-* plus infinitive, see §25.18.

68. The double use of the conjunction *-a* (geminating) means 'both . . . and'. For the spelling, see §1.149, end.

69. Both *kunanza* and *appanza* should be understood as collectives, and *mekki* is predicatival 'much'. Idiomatic English demands plurals: 'Those slain are many . . .'.

70. This sentence is addressed to an angry deity. Note the implication of *kāšma* that the offered substitute is on its way (valid even in this adapted version).

71. A local particle (one in the class of *-kkan*) is obligatory with the verb *aššanu-*.

72. The use of the ablative here is essentially instrumental: 'made right with everything' = 'well prepared in every respect'.

◊5.14. ^{d}*Me-ez-zu-ul-la* GAŠAN*=YA A-NA* ^{d}IŠKUR-*za*[73] *U A-NA* ^{d}UTU ^{URU}*A-ri-in-na a-aš-ši-ya-an-za* DUMU.MUNUS-*aš*
◊5.15. *nu* KUR ^{URU}*Ul-ma-an ḫar-ni-ik-mi nu-uš-ši-kán pé-e-di-iš-ši* ZÀ.AḪ.LI^{SAR} *šu-ú-ni-ya-mi.*

Broad Transcription

5.1. LUGAL-*uš* LÚ.KÚR-*an* UD.KAM-*az wal(a)ḫzi išpantaz=ma=aš tuzziyazi*
5.2. *weriyanteš ŪL=ya weriyanteš* DINGIR.MEŠ-*eš ANA* SÍSKUR *uwanzi*
5.3. DINGIR.MEŠ-*aš weriyawanzi paiweni ḫantezzi=ma=at* UD-*ti ŪL uwanzi*
5.4. $^{LÚ.MEŠ}$SANGA-*eš* DINGIR.MEŠ-*uš punuššanzi kartimmiyatti=wa peran ŪL uwatteni*
5.5. MU.KAM-*za kuit* LUGAL-*waš* ÉRIN.MEŠ-*ti šer tepaweššanza n=at* ^{URU}*Ḫattuša āppa pānzi*
◊ 5.6. *išpanti=ššan šašti šanezziš tešḫaš antuḫšan pittuliyantan natta ēpzi*
♦ 5.7. *takku* LÚ.ULU$_{19}$.LU-*an kuiški ḫūnikzi t=an ištarnikzi nu apūn šāktāizzi*
5.8. *māḫḫan kiššan ištamašmi* LÚ.KÚR-*aš=wa uezzi nu=za* ÉRIN.MEŠ ANŠE.KUR. RA.MEŠ*=ya ninikmi*
◊ 5.9. *nu=za* LUGAL-*uš* ^{URU}*Tuwanuwan zaḫḫiyawanzi ēpzi*
5.10. *antuḫšeš ḫūmanteš dalugauš* MU.KAM.ḪI.A-*uš dušgarattann=a šanḫanzi*
5.11. EN-*aš kuit mekki kartimmiyawanza nu naḫšaraz* ÌR.MEŠ-*uš ēpzi*
5.12. LUGAL-*uš=za ŠA* LÚ.KÚR ÉRIN.MEŠ-*an taruḫzi nu kunanzašš=a mekki* ^{LÚ}*appanzašš=a mekki*
◊5.13. *nu=tta kāšma tarpaššan unuwandan piyami n=aš=kan ḫūmandaz aššanuwanza*
◊5.14. ^{d}*Mezzulla* GAŠAN*=YA ANA* ^{d}IŠKUR*=za U ANA* ^{d} UTU ^{URU}*Arinna āššiyanza* DUMU.MUNUS-*aš*
◊5.15. *nu* KUR ^{URU}*Ulman ḫarnikmi nu=šši=kan pēdi=šši* ZÀ.AḪ.LI^{SAR} *šūniyami*

Vocabulary

āššiyant- 'dear, beloved'
ḫarnink- 'to destroy' (with or without *arḫa*)
ḫūmant- 'all, whole' (usually follows its head noun, but see §§18.8–18.9)
ḫūnink- 'to injure'
išpant- (GE$_{6}$-*ant-*) (comm.) 'night'
ištamašš- 'to hear, listen to'
ištarnink- 'to make sick, incapacitate'
kartimmiyatt- (TUKU.TUKU-*(at)t-*) (comm.) 'anger'
kartimmiyawant- (TUKU.TUKU-*(w)ant-*) 'angry'

73. Recall the function of post-OH *-za* in nominal sentences (§28.37) and note also the implication of its position for the syntactic interpretation of ^{d}*Me-ez-zu-ul-la* GAŠAN*=YA* (§16.10).

mekki 'very' (as degree adverb)
^{d}*Mezzulla-* (comm.) (a deity)
naḫšaratt- (comm.) 'fear, awe; fearsomeness'
nínink- 'to raise, mobilize; (re)move'
pittuliyant- 'worried, anxious'
piya- 'to send'
šāktāi- 'to tend to, care for' (the sick or injured)
šanezzi- 'fine; sweet'
šanḫ- 'to seek; search; sweep'
šašt- (comm.) 'bed; sleep'
šer 'above; on; for' (with preceding dative-locative)
šīwatt- (UD/UD.KAM-(*at*)*t-*) (comm.) 'day' (§4.95)
šūniya- 'to sow, scatter, sprinkle'
ta (conj.) (Old Hittite only; for its use, see §§29.10–29.13)
takku 'if' (Old Hittite only)
daluki- 'long' (§4.38)
tarpašša- (comm.) 'ritual substitute'
tepawešš- 'to become (too) small'
tešḫa- (comm.) (Ù) 'dream'
dušgaratt- (comm.) 'joy'
tuzziya- 'to encamp, make camp, go into camp'
unu- 'to adorn' (also inflected as a stem *unuwāi-*)
wētt-/wītt- (MU/MU.KAM-*t-*) (comm.) 'year' (see §4.95)
zaḫḫiya- 'to fight'
ÉRIN.MEŠ-*t-* (comm.) 'troops'[74]
GAŠAN (comm.) 'lady'
^{d}IŠKUR (comm.) 'Storm-god'
^{d}UTU ^{URU}*Arinna* (comm.) 'Sun-goddess of Arinna'
ZÀ.AḪ.LI^{SAR} (neut.) 'weeds'
U (written with the sign Ù) 'and, but'

74. This noun is grammatically singular but collective in meaning, and Hittite sometimes refers back to it with plural pronouns.

Lesson 6

Grammar

This lesson introduces noun stems in *-r/-n-*, the verb *ḫar(k)-* 'to hold, have' and the present indicative of *mi*-verbs with alternating stem in *-e-/-a-* and verbal stems with the suffix *-ške-*.

One large class of **neuter** nouns in Hittite shows an *r*-suffix in the nominative-accusative but an *-n-* suffix in all the other cases ("heteroclites"—§4.100). The very productive suffixes *-ātar/-ann-* and *-eššar/-eššn-*(/ssn/) form very regular paradigms. Memorize those for *paprātar* 'impurity' (§4.106) and *ḫanneššar* 'legal case' (§4.112). Learn also the similar paradigms of *mēḫur* 'time' (§4.103, end) and *ḫuitar* 'wild animals' (§4.110). A small set of nouns shows variation in the first syllable of their stem in addition to the alternation between *r* and *n*. Memorize the paradigms for *ēšḫar* 'blood', *paḫḫur* 'fire', *uttar* 'word; matter' and *wātar* 'water' (§4.103), paying special attention to the difference between nominative-accusative singular and plural. Verbal nouns in *-war* (i.e., the "verbal substantive") show *-war* in the nominative-accusative and *-waš* in the genitive, with no trace of *-n-* (§4.118). For the use of the verbal substantive, study §§25.3–25.7. While the paradigm of *per* 'house' is unique, it resembles that of *r/n*-stems enough to be conveniently learned here (§4.119).

The verb *ḫar(k)-* 'to hold, have' loses its final *-k-* before endings beginning with a consonant. Memorize only the **present tense** portion of the paradigm (§12.10). Besides functioning as an ordinary main verb 'to hold, have', *ḫar*(*k*)- also occurs in a construction with the nominative-accusative singular neuter form of the participle. Read §§22.19–22.21 and §22.23–22.24 on the two different meanings of this construction.

For *mi*-verbs with truly alternating stems in *-e/a-*, read §12.19 and study only the **present tense** portion of the table found in §12.21. For stems in *-e/u/a-*, memorize the **present tense** paradigm of *uwate-* 'to lead hither' in §12.23, and for those in *-i/u/a-*, memorize that of *zinni-* 'to finish' in §12.26. Also learn the **present tense** of the irregular verb *tē-/tar-* 'say' (§12.46). Read §12.3 for a description of the formation of stems in *-ške-* (but do **not** try to master the details) and memorize the **present tense** forms of *daške-* 'take' (§12.33). The function of verbal stems in *-ške-* (and alternates that need not concern you at this point) is very broad. Learn the basics of their use by reading §§24.9–24.20, but you need only gain an impression of their range of use. Footnotes will aid in recognizing which meaning is intended in a particular example.

Translation Exercise

6.1. *ma-a-an* DINGIR.MEŠ *an-tu-uḫ-ša-an i-da-a-la-wa-az ud-da-na-az Ú-UL pa-aḫ-ša-an-zi na-aš ḫar-ak-zi*

♦ 6.2. LÚ.MEŠ KUR [URU]*Mi-iz-ra-ma ma-aḫ-ḫa-an ŠA* KUR [URU]*Am-ka* GUL-*aḫ-ḫu-wa-ar iš-ta-ma-aš-ša-an-zi na-at na-aḫ-ša-ri-ya-an-zi*[75]

◊ 6.3. *nu-za* DINGIR.MEŠ *i-da-a-la-u-az ud-da-na-az e-eš-ḫa-na-az iš-ḫa-aḫ-ru-wa-az ḫu-u-ma-an-da-az-zi-ya pár-ku-wa-e-eš*[76]

♦ 6.4. *ták-ku* ÌR-*aš* É-*er lu-uk-ke-ez-zi iš-ḫa-a-aš-ši-ša*[77] *še-e-er-ši-it*[78] *šar-ni-ik-zi . . . ták-ku na-at-ta-ma šar-ni-ik-zi nu a-pu-u-un-pát*[79] *šu-ú-ez-zi*

◊ 6.5. *ḫal-ki-iš-wa ma-aḫ-ḫa-an* DUMU.NAM.LÚ.U$_{19}$.LU GUD UDU *ḫu-i-tar-ra ḫu-u-ma-an ḫu-iš-nu-uš-ke-ez-zi*[80] LUGAL MUNUS.LUGAL *ki-i-ya*[81] É-*er ka-a-aš*[81] *ḫal-ki-iš kal-la-ri-it*[82] *ud-da-na-az QA-TAM-MA ḫu-iš-nu-zi*

6.6. DINGIR.MEŠ-*aš* [UZU]*šu-up-pa pa-aḫ-ḫu-e-ni-it za-nu-me-ni nu* EGIR-*an-da pa-aḫ-ḫur ú-i-te-ni-it ki-iš-ta-nu-me-ni*

♦ 6.7. TI-*an-za-aš*[83] *nu* [d]UTU *ŠA-ME-E* IGI.ḪI.A-*it uš-ke-ez-zi* NINDA-*an-na-az*[84] TI-*an-na-aš az-zi-ik-ke-ez-zi*

6.8. *ne-ku-uz me-e-ḫur* UN.MEŠ-*eš ḫu-u-ma-an-te-eš pár-na pa-a-an-zi*

6.9. [LÚ]AZU *ŠA* EN.SÍSKUR É-*er iš-ḫa-na-az pa-ap-ra-an-na-az-zi-ya pár-ku-nu-zi*

◊6.10. [LÚ]AZU-*aš-ta ḫa-a-aš-ša-an a-ra-aḫ-za-an-da ši-i-eš-ni-it gul-aš-zi*

6.11. DINGIR.MEŠ *ta-ra-an-te-eš Ú-UL-ya ta-ra-an-te-eš a-ru-na-az* ḪUR.SAG.MEŠ-*az ḫa-a-ri-ya-az ú-el-lu-wa-az pé-e-da-az-zi-ya ḫu-u-ma-an-da-az ú-wa-an-zi*

6.12. LUGAL-*wa-aš* LÚ.MEŠ KÚR*=ŠU ḫu-u-ma-an-du-uš ḫu-ul-la-mi nu* KUR-*SÚ ḫu-u-ma-an-da-az pa-aḫ-ḫa-aš-mi*

◊6.13. [m]*Zu-ru-uš* GAL LÚ.MEŠ *ME-ŠE-DI du-ud-du-mi-li ḫa-aš-ša-an-na-aš-ša-aš*[104] DUMU*=ŠU* [m]*Ta-ḫur-wa-i-li-in pí-i-e-ez-zi nu-za-kán* [m]*Ti-it-ti-ya-aš ḫa-aš-ša-tar ku-en-zi*

6.14. LUGAL-*uš-za* KUR.KUR.MEŠ LÚ.KÚR *tar-uḫ-ḫa-an ḫar-zi*[85]

75. See §22.14.

76. NB the presence of *-za* in a nominal sentence!

77. The enclitic *-šiš* is a possessive adjective meaning 'his' (likewise *-šaš* in sentence 13). For the final *-a*, see §28.155, end.

78. For the grammar of *šēr=šit*, see §6.6 and §20.31. The sense of the postposition here is 'for'.

79. *apūn* is acc. sg. comm. of the anaphoric pronoun *apā-*, thus 'him', referring back to ÌR-*aš*. The force of the particle here is well expressed in English by 'the very same' (and no one else).

80. The *-ške-*form marks omnitemporality here. The statement is "gnomic," i.e., true at any time (§24.17).

81. *kī* (nom.-acc. sg.neut.) and *kāš* (nom. sg.comm.) both mean 'this'. The coordinated direct object has been topicalized (§30.28).

82. For this erroneous use of the instrumental for an ablative in a copy, see §16.103.

83. This word is a complete nominal sentence. The reference is to a priestess removed from her office but spared the death penalty for committing murder and thus still able to enjoy life.

84. For the alternate writing of *-za*, see §28.19. The unexpected word order of head noun + genitive is likely due to topicalization (cf. §30.32).

85. Without context one cannot determine whether this is an analytic perfect or a stative construction, but the context of similar real examples argues for the latter. The ideal was that the Hittite king kept the lands he overcame under his power (even if this was not always true).

♦6.15. *ḫar-na-u-aš-za ku-it* MUNUS-*za*[86] *A-NA* DINGIR-*LÌ* EN-*YA še-er* SAG.DU-*za šar-ni-in-kán ḫar-mi*

Broad Transcription

6.1. *mān* DINGIR.MEŠ *antuḫšan idālawaz uddanaz ŪL paḫšanzi n=aš ḫar(a)kzi*

♦ 6.2. LÚ.MEŠ KUR ^{URU}*Mizra=ma maḫḫan ŠA* KUR ^{URU}*Amka* GUL-*aḫḫuwar ištamaššanzi n=at naḫšariyanzi*

◊ 6.3. *nu=za* DINGIR.MEŠ *idālawaz uddanaz ēšḫanaz išḫaḫruwaz ḫūmandazzi=ya parkuwaēš*

♦ 6.4. *takku* ÌR-*aš* É-*er lukkezzi išḫāš=šiš=a šēr=šit šarnikzi . . . takku natta=ma šarnikzi nu apūn=pat šuwezzi*

◊ 6.5. *ḫalkiš=wa maḫḫan* DUMU.NAM.LÚ.U$_{19}$.LU GUD UDU *ḫuitarr=a ḫūman ḫuišnuškezzi* LUGAL MUNUS.LUGAL *kī=ya* É-*er kāš ḫalkiš kallarit uddanaz QATAMMA ḫuišnuzi*

6.6. DINGIR.MEŠ-*aš* ^{UZU}*šuppa paḫḫuenit zanumeni nu* EGIR-*anda paḫḫur witenit kištanumeni*

♦ 6.7. TI-*anza=aš nu* ^{d}UTU *ŠAMÊ* IGI.ḪI.A-*it uškezzi* NINDA-*ann=a=z* TI-*annaš azzikkezzi*

6.8. *nekuz meḫur* UN.MEŠ-*eš ḫūmanteš parna pānzi*

6.9. ^{LÚ}AZU *ŠA* EN.SÍSKUR É-*er išḫanaz paprannazzi=ya parkunuzi*

◊6.10. ^{LÚ}AZU-*aš=(š)ta ḫāššan araḫzanda šiyešnit gul(a)šzi*

6.11. DINGIR.MEŠ *taranteš ŪL=ya taranteš arunaz* ḪUR.SAG.MEŠ-*az ḫāriyaz welluwaz pēdazzi=ya ḫūmandaz uwanzi*

6.12. LUGAL-*waš* LÚ.MEŠ KÚR=*ŠÚ ḫūmanduš ḫullami nu* KUR=*ŠÚ ḫūmandaz paḫḫašmi*

◊6.13. ^{m}*Zuruš* GAL LÚ.MEŠ *MEŠEDI duddumili ḫaššannaš=šaš* DUMU=*ŠU* ^{m}*Taḫurwailin piyēzzi nu=za=kan* ^{m}*Tittiyaš ḫaššatar kuenzi*

6.14. LUGAL-*uš=za* KUR.KUR.MEŠ LÚ.KÚR *taruḫḫan ḫarzi*

♦6.15. *ḫarnawaš=za kuit* MUNUS-*za ANA* DINGIR-*LÌ* EN=*YA šer* SAG.DU-*za šarninkan ḫarmi*

Vocabulary

appanda (EGIR-(*p*)*anda*) ‘behind; afterwards’
araḫzanda ‘around’
ēšḫar (neut.) ‘blood; bloodshed’
ḫar(k)- ‘to hold; have’
ḫarnāu- (comm.) ‘birthing stool’ (§4.48)

86. The first clause ends with MUNUS-*za*. NB the presence of *-za*! The lack of *nu* introducing the next clause is rather unusual but is attested elsewhere: cf. §30.65. SAG.DU-*za* here means merely ‘personally’; it does not mean that she has paid with her life!

ḫaršar (SAG.DU) (neut.) 'head; person'
ḫaššātar (MÁŠ-*tar*) (neut.) 'birth; family'
ḫuišwant- (TI-(*w*)*ant-*) 'alive, living'
ḫuišwātar (TI-(*wa*)*tar*) (neut.) 'life'
ḫuitar (neut.) 'wild animals'[87]
ḫulli/u/a- 'to fight (someone, -thing); contravene'
išḫaḫru- (neut.) 'tears'
kallar(a)- 'unfavorable, harmful'
kištanu- 'to extinguish'
gul(a)šš- 'to incise, inscribe, draw'
lukke/a- 'to set fire to'
mēḫur (neut.) 'time' (cf. on the syntax §16.25 and note 4 to §16.7)
nekut- (comm.) 'twilight, evening' (see note 353 to §4.94)
paḫ(ḫa)š- 'to protect'
paḫḫur (IZI) (neut.) 'fire'
paprātar (neut.) 'impurity'
parkunu- 'to purify, cleanse'
-pat (a particle) (see §§28.119–28.140)
**pēr* (É) (neut.) 'house'
šākuwi- (IGI-*i-*) (comm.) 'eye'[88]
šarnink- 'to make restitution'
šiyeššar (KAŠ-*eššar*) (neut.) 'beer'
šūwe/a- 'to push (away), reject'
tē-/tar- 'to speak; mention' (§12.46)
duddumili 'secretly'
uške- 'to see' (pluractional stem)
uttar (INIM) (neut.) 'word; matter, affair'
wātar (A) (neut.) 'water'
DUMU.NAM.LÚ.U$_{19}$.LU-(*l*)*a-* (comm.) 'human being'[89]
EN SÍSKUR (comm.) 'client, patron, sacrificer'
GAL LÚ.MES *MEŠEDI* (comm.) 'chief of the bodyguard'
MUNUS-*(n)-* (comm.) 'woman' (for its inflection, see §4.74)
UDU-*u-* (comm.) 'sheep'

87. This noun always has a collective meaning, even in the singular.

88. This noun is a common gender *i*-stem in the singular, but the plural is consistently a collective in -*a*-. See the CHD Š 65–7.

89. This writing stands for Hittite *dandukišnaš* DUMU-*la-* 'son of mortality'. We still do not know the full form of the Hittite word for 'son, child'.

Lesson 7

Grammar

This lesson introduces *n*-stem nouns and the **preterite** tense of *mi*-conjugation verbs.

For neuter *n*-stem nouns, read §§4.64–4.65 and memorize the paradigm of *lāman-* 'name' (§4.66). Also memorize the special paradigm of *tēkan* 'earth' (§4.68), which has a unique stem variation. Most common-gender *n*-stem nouns show variation between a stem without *-n-* in the nominative singular and one with *-n-* elsewhere. Read §§4.69–4.70 and memorize the paradigms of *memi(y)an-* 'word' and *ḫāran-* 'eagle' (§4.71), paying special attention to the tendency of these stems to become *a*-stems. The small class of common-gender nouns in *-anza(n)-* also shows variation between a stem without *-n-* in the nominative singular and one with *-n-* elsewhere. Read carefully the description of this type in §4.75, noting the existence of nom. sg. in *-anza* or *-anzaš*.

Learn the preterite endings of the *mi*-conjugation (§11.6). NB the differences in the endings of the singular for consonant and vocalic stems in OH and the ambiguity of the ending ***-tta*** (unfortunately, in NH the ending ***-t*** of vocalic stems becomes ambiguous as well). Then carefully study the **preterite tense** portions of the paradigms representing all the various classes of *mi*-conjugation verbs whose present tenses were previously learned: *wal(a)ḫ-* (§12.8), *ēpp-* (§12.3), *ēd-* (§12.3), *kuen-* (§12.5), *waḫnu-* (§12.44), *iya-* (§12.29), verbs in *-ešš-* (§12.18), *ḫandāi-* (§12.36), *pai-* and *uwa-* (§12.41), *ḫarnink-* (§12.16), verbs in *-e/a-* (§12.21), *uwate-* (§12.23), *zinni-* (§12.26), *daške-* (§12.33) and *tē-/tar-* (§12.46). Since any stem variation is of the same type as in the present tense, there should be no difficulty in learning the preterite tense for all of these at once (that the distribution among persons differs is immaterial).

Translation Exercise

◊ 7.1. *nu-wa I-NA* KUR ^{URU}*Ḫa-at-ti ḫi-in-kán pí-ya-at-tén*[90] *nu-wa* KUR ^{URU}*Ḫa-at-ti ḫi-in-ga-na-az me-ek-ki ta-ma-aš-ša-an e-eš-ta*[91]

90. This quotation is addressed to the gods in a prayer.

91. Since this clause expresses the result of the preceding, it must be read as a "state" passive, not an "event" passive. Read now §§21.12–21.14. Recall that in NH the ablative can express means and agency (§§16.90–16.91). For the Hittites this one is probably the former, with the gods as the agents who sent it.

◊ 7.2. *ŠA* LÚ.MEŠ IGI.NU.GÁL-*mu ut-tar ḫa-at-ra-a-eš*[92] *na-aš-mu lam-ni-it ḫa-at-ra-a-eš*

♦ 7.3. *nu-kán* LÚ.MEŠ IGI.NU.GÁL.ḪI.A *ḫu-u-ma-an-te-eš*[93] ^{URU}*Ša-pí-nu-wa ša-ra-a pé-ḫu-te-er*

♦ 7.4. *ú-i-il-na-aš* ÉRIN.MEŠ-*an te-eš-šu-um-mi-uš-ša ta-ak-na-a ḫa-ri-e-mi tu-uš tar-ma-e-mi*

♦ 7.5. *a-še-eš-šar ša-ra-a ti-ya-zi nu* $^{\text{LÚ.MEŠ}}$ZABAR.DAB *a-še-eš-ni a-ku-wa-an-na pí-an-zi*[94]

♦ 7.6. ^{URU}*Kap-pé-e-ri-in-ma-za* ^{URU}*Ka-a-ra-aš-šu-wa-an* ^{URU}*Ḫar-na-an-na ar-kam-ma-na-aš*[95] *i-ya-nu-un nu* ^{URU}*Ḫa-at-tu-ši* GEŠTIN-*an ar-kam-ma-na-an-ni pé-e ḫar-ker*

♦ 7.7. GUD-*un-aš-ta*[96] *ḫa-a-li-az a-ap-pa Ú-UL ku-uš-ša-an-ka kar-šu-un*[97] UDU-*un-aš-ta*[96] *a-ša-ú-na-az* EGIR-*pa* KI.MIN[98]

♦ 7.8. *A-NA* DUMU.NAM.LÚ.U_{19}.LU-*pát-kán*[99] *an-da me-mi-an kiš-an me-mi-iš-kán-zi ḫar-na-a-u-wa-aš-wa* MUNUS-*ni-i* DINGIR-*LU_4 ka-a-ri ti-ya-zi*

◊ 7.9. ^{m}*Ḫa-an-ti-li-ša*[100] ^{LÚ}SAGI.A-*aš e-eš-ta nu-za* ^{f}*Ḫa-ra-ap-ši-li-in* NIN ^{m}*Mur-ši-i-li* DAM-*an-ni ḫar-ta*

♦7.10. KUR ^{URU}*Ḫa-pa-al-la-ma-az*[101] *li-in-ki-ya*[102] *kat-ta-an ki-iš-ša-an*[103] *zi-ik-ke-eš . . . nam-ma-ma-kán* KUR ^{URU}*Ḫa-pa-a-al-la ku-en-ta-ya Ú-UL*[104] *e-ep-ta-ya-at Ú-UL*[104]

7.11. *NI-IŠ* DINGIR.MEŠ-*kán*[105] *ḫu-u-ma-an-te-eš* ḪUL-*un* UN-*an da-an-ku-ya-az ták-na-az ar-ḫa ḫar-ni-in-ker*

7.12. LÚ.KÚR-*aš I-NA* KUR-*TÌ an-da ú-et nu* $^{\text{A.ŠÀ}}$*ku-e-ru-uš lu-uk-ke-et nu ḫal-ki-uš ḫu-u-ma-an-du-uš ḫar-ni-ik-ta*

92. Sentence 7.3 follows the real version of sentence 7.2 in a letter addressed by one official to another.

93. In this MH text the nom. pl. comm. ending *-eš* is being used for the accusative (see Hoffner 2010b: 120 §57 and in this grammar §3.17.

94. *pianzi* is present third person plural '(they) give'.

95. The genitive *arkammanaš* means here 'tribute-bearing' (see §16.46), and the reflexive means '(I made them tributary) to myself'.

96. For the significance of the syllabification of GUD-*un-aš-ta*, see §1.13. For the particle *-ašta* underscoring separation, see §28.65.

97. The context is a prayer in which the speaker is denying that he held back (*āppa*) choice animals from offerings to the gods for his own use.

98. KI.MIN functions like English 'ditto'—that is, the scribe uses KI.MIN to indicate repetition of whatever has not changed in the preceding text of parallel constructions. Here (in ♦7.7) it stands for *ŪL kuššanka karšun*.

99. The particle *-kkan* here underscores the local sense of 'among mankind'. See §28.90. The force of *-pat* is likely counterexpectational (§28.140). Thus CHD P 225b 10 b 2′.

100. The sentence in its original context introduces this person as a new topic, hence the contrastive focus particle *-a*, which is untranslatable in this case (see §28.155, end). On its form, see §29.30.

101. Read as *=ma=z*, with the conjunction *-ma* (untranslatable out of context) and the reflexive particle *-z(a)*.

102. *linkiya* is d.-l. singular of *lingai-* 'oath'. On the functions of the ending *-a* in *i*-stems, cf. §3.28 with note 61.

103. *kiššan* 'as follows' refers to a following direct quotation in the original text that is omitted here.

104. The combination of double *=ya* 'also, and' and the negative is equivalent to 'neither . . . nor'. You should assume that *kuenta* and *ēpta* are the same person and number as *zikkeš*. The force of *-ške-* here is iterative.

105. For the use of *-kkan* with *ḫarnink-*, see §28.114.

♦7.13. *na-aš-ta*[106] É-*ri an-da la-aḫ-ḫa-an-za-na-aš*^{MUŠEN} *ḫi-<im->mu-uš i-ya-an-zi nu ŠA* GIŠ.ḪI.A 10 *la-<aḫ->ḫa-an-za*^{MUŠEN}[107] *i-ya-an-za nu-uš IŠ-TU* KÙ.BABBAR *ḫa-liš-ši-ya-an-zi*

7.14. ^{d}UTU-*uš ḫa-a-ra-na-an*^{MUŠEN} *le-e-li-wa-an-da-an pí-i-e-et na-aš-ta pár-ga-mu-uš* ḪUR.SAG.ḪI.A-*uš ša-an-aḫ-ta* ^{d}*Te-li-pí-nu-na*[108] *Ú-UL ú-e-mi-ya-at*

7.15. LUGAL-*uš* $^{\text{LÚ.MEŠ}}$*ḫa-lu-kat-tal-la-aš te-ez-zi ku-wa-at-wa ú-wa-at-tén nu-uš-ši a-ap-pa ta-ra-an-zi ták-šu-la-an-na-aš-wa-at-ta me-mi-ni še-er ú-wa-u-en*

Broad Transcription

◊7.1. *nu⸗wa INA* KUR ^{URU}*Ḫatti ḫinkan piyatten nu⸗wa* KUR ^{URU}*Ḫatti ḫinganaz mekki tamaššan ēšta* ◊7.2. *ŠA* LÚ.MEŠ IGI.NU.GÁL⸗*mu uttar ḫatrāeš n⸗aš⸗mu lamnit ḫatrāeš* ♦7.3. *nu⸗kán* LÚ.MEŠ IGI.NU.GÁL.ḪI.A *ḫūmanteš* ^{URU}*Šapinuwa šarā peḫuter* ♦7.4. *wīlnaš* ÉRIN.MEŠ-*an teššummiušš⸗a taknā ḫariemi t⸗uš tar-maemi* ♦7.5. *ašeššar šarā tiyazi nu* $^{\text{LÚ.MEŠ}}$ZABAR.DAB *ašešni akuwanna pianzi* ♦7.6. ^{URU}*Kappērin⸗ma⸗za* ^{URU}*Kāraššuwan* ^{URU}*Ḫarnann⸗a arkammanaš iyanun nu* ^{URU}*Ḫattuši* GEŠTIN-*an arkammananni pē ḫarker* ♦7.7. GUD-*un⸗ašta ḫāliaz āppa ŪL kuššanka karšun* UDU-*un⸗ašta ašaunaz* EGIR-*pa* KI.MIN ♦7.8. *ANA* DUMU.NAM.LÚ.U$_{19}$.LU⸗*pat⸗kan anda memian kišan memiškanzi ḫarnāuwaš⸗wa* MUNUS-*nī* DINGIR-*LU*$_4$ *kāri tiyazi* ◊7.9. ^{m}*Ḫantiliš⸗a* ^{LÚ}SAGI.A-*aš ēšta nu⸗za* ^{f}*Ḫarapšilin* NIN ^{m}*Muršīli* DAM-*anni ḫarta* ♦7.10. KUR ^{URU}*Ḫapalla⸗ma⸗z linkiya kat-tan kiššan zikkeš* ... *namma⸗ma⸗kan* KUR ^{URU}*Ḫapālla kuenta⸗ya ŪL ēpta⸗ya⸗at ŪL* 7.11. *NIŠ* DINGIR.MEŠ⸗*kan ḫūmanteš* ḪUL-*un* UN-*an dankuyaz taknaz arḫa ḫarninker* 12. LÚ.KÚR-*aš INA* KUR-*TÌ anda uet nu* $^{\text{LÚ.MEŠ}}$SANGA-*aš* $^{\text{A.ŠÀ}}$*kueruš luk-ket nu ḫalkiuš ḫūmanduš ḫarnikta* ♦7.13. *n⸗ašta* É-*ri anda laḫḫanzanaš*^{MUŠEN} *ḫimmuš iyanzi nu ŠA* GIŠ.ḪI.A 10 *laḫḫanza*^{MUŠEN} *iyanza n⸗uš IŠTU* KÙ.BABBAR *ḫališšiyanzi* 7.14. ^{d}UTU-*uš ḫāranan*^{MUŠEN} *lēliwandan piyet n⸗ašta pargamuš* ḪURSAG.ḪI.A-*uš šan(a)ḫta* ^{d}*Telipinun⸗a ŪL wemiyat* 7.15. LUGAL-*uš* $^{\text{LÚ.MEŠ}}$*ḫalukattallaš tezzi kuwat⸗wa uwatten nu⸗šši āppa taranzi takšulannaš⸗wa⸗tta memini šer uwawen*

Vocabulary

anda (postposition with d.-l.) 'in, among'
arkam(m)an- (comm.) 'tribute'
arkam(m)anātar (neut.) 'payment of tribute'
ašāwar (TÙR) (neut.) 'sheepfold' (see §4.115)

106. The local particle *-ašta* often associates with the adverb/postposition *anda* in the same clause. But the exact sense of this is still unclear.

107. Hittite often uses a singular noun with a number higher than one. See §9.18 and following. Since this clause is parallel to the preceding, it is surely to be read as an event passive. Cf. note 91 above.

108. Note that the conjunction is non-geminating *-a* (i.e., *-a/-ma* marking contrastive topics, §29.35), hence 'but' in this context.

ašeššar (neut.) ‘assembly’
ḫāli- (neut.) ‘corral’
ḫališšiya- ‘to coat, plate, inlay’
^{LÚ}*ḫalugattalla-* (LÚ *ṬĒME*) (comm.) ‘messenger’
ḫāran-^{MUŠEN} ($\text{TI}_8^{\text{MUŠEN}}$) (comm.) ‘eagle’
ḫariya- ‘to bury’
ḫenkan- (ÚŠ) (neut.) ‘death; plague’
ḫimma- (comm.) ‘model, replica’
kāri tiya- ‘to accede to (the wishes of)’
karš- ‘to cut; segregate’
kattan (GAM-*an*) ‘under’
kuššanka ‘ever’, *kuššanka* + *natta* = ‘never’
laḫ(ḫ)anzan-^{MUŠEN} (comm.) (kind of duck)
lāman (*ŠUM-an*) (neut.) ‘name’
lēliwant- ‘swift’
linkiyanteš (*NIŠ* DINGIR.MEŠ) ‘the oaths’ (as individuated agents of retribution, but not a fully grammaticalized ergative; cf. §§3.8-3.11)[109]
memi(y)an- (INIM) (comm.) ‘word; matter, affair’
memiške- ‘to say, speak’
nega- (NIN-*a-*) (comm.) ‘sister’
pē ḫar(k)- ‘to offer, furnish’
peḫute- ‘to lead’ (see §12.23)
takšulatar (neut.) ‘peace’
tamašš- ‘to press, oppress’
tēkan (KI) (neut.) ‘earth’
^{d}*Telipinu-* (comm.) (a male deity of the storm-god class, generally conceived as the producer of life and proliferation among plants and animals)
te/iššummi- (GAL-*i-*) (comm.) ‘cup’
wil(a)n- (IM) (comm.) ‘clay’
zikke- ‘to place’ (pluractional stem)
DAM-*atar* (neut.) ‘wifehood, marriage’
GUD (or GU_4)-*u-* (comm.) ‘bovine, cow, steer’
KI.MIN (functions like English ‘ditto’); see note 124 above)
KÙ.BABBAR-*i-* (neut.) ‘silver’
LÚ IGI.NU.GÁL (comm.) ‘blind man’
^{LÚ}SAGI(.A)-*(l)a-* (comm.) ‘cupbearer’
^{LÚ}ZABAR.DAB (comm.) (an offical who distributes beverages)

109. Not to be confused with DINGIR.MEŠ *MAMITI* = *linkiyaš* DINGIR.MEŠ ‘gods of the oath’, who are the *named* deities in treaties who are called to witness the oaths. Cf. sentence 14 in lesson 14.

Lesson 8

Grammar

This lesson introduces nominal stems in *-l-*, *-r-* and *-š-* and the present indicative of consonantal stems of the *ḫi*-conjugation. Nouns in *-al* and *-ul* are neuters; read §§4.59–4.60 and §§4.62 and memorize the paradigms of *ḫāḫḫal-* 'bush' and *išḫiul-* 'obligation'. Some stems in *-īl* are neuter, while others appear to be common gender, but note that in both cases the nominative and accusative singular may have a zero ending (memorize the paradigms of *alil-* 'blossom' (comm.) and *šuwīl-* 'thread' in §4.61). Most nouns in *-ur* are neuter; read §4.85 and memorize the paradigm of *aniur* 'ritual' (§4.86). The old noun *kūrur-* 'enmity' is also attested as a predicate adjective (study the paradigm in §4.86). Nouns and adjectives in *-ar* may be common gender or neuter. Both genders show nominative and accusative singulars with zero ending, but there is a strong tendency for the common gender nouns to be inflected as *a*-stems. Read §4.78 and study the paradigms of *ḫūppar-* 'bowl' (comm.), *šittar-* 'sun-disk' (comm.), *ḫāppar-* 'purchase, sale' (neut.) (§4.79) and the adjective *šakuwaššar-* 'full, complete' (§4.81). The word for 'hand' already learned as an *a*-stem also shows traces of its original inflection as an *r*-stem with an alternating stem. Study the paradigm in §4.80. Most *š*-stem nouns are neuter and have an invariant stem; read §4.87 and memorize the paradigm of *nēpiš-* 'heaven, sky' (§4.88, end). The noun for 'mouth' shows stem variation; learn the paradigm of *aiš/išš-* in §4.88. The type in §4.89 may be ignored for now.

Learn the present tense endings of the *ḫi*-conjugation (§11.6), ignoring rare variants in parentheses and footnotes. Some consonantal stems of the *ḫi*-conjugation show an invariant stem or only quantitative allomorphy *ā/a*, while others show an alternation between *ā* in the singular and *e* in the plural. Note that this distribution is the **opposite** of that for corresponding verbs of the *mi*-conjugation. Memorize the **present tense** portion of the paradigms of *ār-/ar-* 'to arrive' and *šākk-/šekk-* 'to know' (§13.1) and *šipā/and-/išpā/and-* 'to libate' (§13.3). Note that some verbs ending in a single consonant show an alternation between simple consonant in the third person singular and geminate consonant in the third person plural (*aki* vs. *akkanzi* in §13.3).

Translation Exercise

♦ 8.1. *nu-kán A-NA* ALAM 1 GUD.NIGA 7 UDU.ḪI.A-*ya ši-pa-an-da-an-zi*[110] 1 UDU *ták-na-aš* ^{d}UTU-*i* 1 UDU ^{d}UTU *ŠA-ME-E* 2 UDU *ḫu-uḫ-ḫa-aš ḫa-an-na-aš* 2 UDU 1 GUD.NIGA *ak-kán-ta-aš* ZI-*ni* 1 UDU-*ma-kán A-NA* ^{d}UD.SIG$_5$ *ši-pa-an-da-an-zi*

◊ 8.2. *nu-uš-ma-aš*[111] ^{d}IŠKUR ^{URU}*Ḫa-at-ti iš-ḫi-ú-ul A-NA* LÚ.MEŠ ^{URU}*Ḫa-at-ti me-na-aḫ-ḫa-an-da i-ya-at*

♦ 8.3. LUGAL-*uš ḫu-u-up-pa-ri ši-pa-an-ti* MUNUS.LUGAL-*ša na-at-ta*

8.4. ^{LÚ}SANGA-*iš* NINDA-*an ku-un-ni-it ki-iš-šar-ta e-ep-ta na-an* DINGIR-*LÌ-ni pé-e ḫar-ta*

8.5. *an-tu-uḫ-ša-aš-kán*[112] *an-da me-mi-iš-kán-zi ŠA A-BI-ŠU-wa-kán wa-aš-túl A-NA* DUMU-*ŠU a-ri*

♦ 8.6. *ták-ku* MUNUS-[*za ḫ*]*a-a-ši nu an-na-az-pát*[113] ŠÀ-*az* [*a-*]*i-iš ar-ḫa ḫa-a-ši nu me-ma-i*[114] ^{d}10-*aš* KUR-*e za-a-ḫi*[115]

♦ 8.7. *ták-ku* LÚ ^{GIŠ}TUKUL-*aš* A.ŠÀ.ḪI.A-*ŠU ḫu-u-ma-an-da-an ku-iš-ki*[116] *wa-a-ši lu-uz-zi kar-pí-ez-zi*

♦ 8.8. ^{URU}*Kat-ti-ti-mu-wa-aš-ma-mu ták-šu-ul e-eš-ta na-an-kán iš-tar-na ar-ḫa pa-a-un nu* KUR ^{URU}*Tág-ga-aš-ta* GUL-*aḫ-ḫu-un*

◊ 8.9. *nu-mu* KUR ^{URU}*Pí-ig-ga-i-na-re-eš-ša ku-it ku-u-ru-ur e-eš-ta nu-uš-ša-an*[117] *pa-a-un* KUR ^{URU}*Pí-ig-ga-i-na-re-eš-ša ša-aš-ti wa-al-aḫ-ḫu-un*

◊8.10. MUNUS ŠU.GI GÙB-*la-az*[118] ^{TÚG}*ku-re-eš-šar*$^{\text{ḪI.A}}$ *A-NA* ^{GIŠ}BANŠUR *pé-ra-an kat-ta ga-an-ki*

◊ 8.11. *ma-aḫ-ḫa-an-ma I-NA* ^{URU}*Tar-ku-ma a-ar-ḫi nu* ^{URU}*Tar-ku-ma-an ar-ḫa wa-ar-nu-mi*

♦8.12. *ša-ra-a-kán ú-wa-ši*[119] *ne-pí-ša-aš* ^{d}UTU-*uš a-ru-na-az nu-uš-ša-an ne-pí-ši ti-ya-ši*

♦8.13. *nu* ZAG *še-ek-kán-te-et*[120] ZI-*it an-da le-e ku-iš-ki*[116] *za-a-ḫi*

110. What follows *ši-pa-an-da-an-zi* here is a detailed enumeration of the animal offerings. The first seven are treated as an "extraposed" apposition (§30.26). The last contrasting 1 UDU-*ma-kán* is treated as a new clause. It may have been added when the scribe realized that one sheep and one deity had been omitted.

111. The reference is to the Egyptians.

112. See note 99 above to sentence 7.8.

113. The sense of *-pát* here is 'right (from)'. For the ablative *annaz*, see §§16.19 and 16.86.

114. *memai* is pres. 3 sg. 'speaks'. The subject is the newborn child.

115. The sense of the present tense here is future. This is not what the newborn says but a prediction based upon this omen.

116. *kuiški* (nom. sg. comm.) is 'someone'. Combined with the negative in sentence 8.13 it means 'no one'.

117. For the use of *-(š)šan*, see §28.74 (as in English 'upon one's bed' vs. 'in bed'), and for its position, §24.28.

118. As is usual for ZAG-*az* or GÙB-*laz* alone, this is an adverb 'on/to the left', indicating relative location (§16.83).

119. Appearance of both the preverb and finite verb clause-initially is virtually unique and not in accordance with the rules of Hittite grammar. We are surely dealing with a foreign source and translationese (cf. Singer 1996: 180–81). The nominative noun phrase is in apposition to the subject (§16.11).

120. The participle here has an active sense 'knowing'. See §25.36, end.

◊8.14. *ne-pí-ša-aš* ^{d}UTU-*uš* DINGIR.MEŠ *ḫu-u-ma-an-du-uš ne-pí-ša-az ták-na-a-az* ḪUR.SAG.MEŠ-*az* ÍD.MEŠ-*az IŠ-TU* É.MEŠ DINGIR.MEŠ-*ŠU-NU ú-e-ri-ya-at*

◊8.15. *ták-ku ḫa-an-ne-eš-na-aš iš-ḫa-a-aš*[121] *le-e-la-ni-at-ta*[122] *šar-ti-an-na wa-al-aḫ-zi na-aš a-ki šar-ni-ik-zi-il* NU.GÁL

Broad Transcription

♦ 8.1. *nu≈kan ANA* ALAM 1 GUD.NIGA 7 UDU.ḪI.A*≈ya šipandanzi* 1 UDU *taknaš* ^{d}UTU-*i* 1 UDU ^{d}UTU *ŠAMÊ* 2 UDU *ḫuḫḫaš ḫannaš* 2 UDU 1 GUD.NIGA *akkantaš* ZI-*ni* 1 UDU*≈ma≈kan ANA* ^{d}UD.SIG$_5$ *šipandanzi*

◊ 8.2. *nu≈šmaš* ^{d}IŠKUR ^{URU}*Ḫatti išḫiūl ANA* LÚ.MEŠ ^{URU}*Ḫatti menaḫḫanda iyat*

♦ 8.3. LUGAL-*uš ḫūppari šipanti* MUNUS.LUGAL-*š≈a natta*

8.4. ^{LÚ}SANGA-*iš* NINDA-*an kunnit kiššarta ēpta n≈an* DINGIR-*LÌ-ni pē ḫarta*

8.5. *antuḫšaš≈kan anda memiškanzi ŠA ABI≈ŠU≈wa≈kan waštul ANA* DUMU*≈ŠU ari*

♦ 8.6. *takku* MUNUS-*za ḫāši nu annaz≈pat* ŠÀ-*az aīš arḫa ḫāši nu memai* ^{d}10-*aš* KUR-*e zāḫi*

♦ 8.7. *takku* LÚ ^{GIŠ}TUKUL-*aš* A.ŠÀ.ḪI.A*≈ŠU ḫūmandan kuiški wāši luzzi karpiezzi*

♦ 8.8. ^{URU}*Kattitimuwaš≈ma≈mu takšul ēšta n≈an≈kan ištarna arḫa pāun nu* KUR ^{URU}*Taggašta* GUL-*aḫḫun*

◊ 8.9. *nu≈mu* KUR ^{URU}*Piggainarešša kuit kūrur ēšta nu≈ššan pāun* KUR ^{URU}*Piggainarešša šašti wal(a)ḫḫun*

◊8.10. MUNUS ŠU.GI GÙB-*laz* ^{TÚG}*kureššar*$^{\text{ḪI.A}}$ *ANA* ^{GIŠ}BANŠUR *peran katta ganki*

◊ 8.11. *maḫḫan≈ma INA* ^{URU}*Tarkuma ārḫi nu* ^{URU}*Tarkuman arḫa warnumi*

♦8.12. *šarā≈kan uwaši nepišaš* ^{d}UTU-*uš arunaz nu≈ššan nepiši tiyaši*

♦8.13. *nu* ZAG *šekkantet* ZI-*it anda lē kuiški zāḫi*

◊8.14. *nepišaš* ^{d}UTU-*uš* DINGIR.MEŠ *ḫūmanduš nepišaz taknāz* ḪUR.SAG.MEŠ-*az* ÍD.MEŠ-*az IŠTU* É.MEŠ DINGIR.MEŠ*≈ŠUNU weriyat*

♦8.15. *takku ḫannešnaš išḫāš lēlaniatta šartiann≈a wal(a)ḫzi n≈aš aki šarnikzil* NU.GÁL

Vocabulary

aiš- (KA×U-*iš*) (neut.) ‘mouth’ (cf. §4.88)
āk-/akk-^{ḫḫi} ‘to die’[123]

121. The ‘lord/master of the law case’ is a ‘litigant’ or ‘opponent in court’, a calque of Akkadian *BĒL DĪNI* (§32.38).

122. The verb *lēlaniatta* (medio-passive pres. 3 sg.) means ‘becomes furious’. The clause *n≈aš aki* is another instance where *nu* may have the force of ‘so that’ (cf. §30.50).

123. From this point on, all verbs belonging to the “*ḫi*-conjugation” will be marked with superscripted ^{ḫḫi} as here.

ā/ar-^{hhi} 'to arrive (at), reach' (+ d.-l. or allative)
ḫanna- (comm.) 'grandmother'
ḫanneššar (DI) (neut.) 'judgment, law case'
ḫapan- (ÍD-*a(n)*-) (comm.) 'river'
ḫāš-/ḫašš- and *ḫeš(š)-*^{hhi} 'to open (tr.)' (with or without the preverb *āppa*)[124]
ḫāš-/ḫašš-^{hhi} 'to give birth'
ḫuḫḫa- (comm.) 'grandfather; forefather'
ḫūppar- (comm.) 'bowl'
išḫiūl- (*RIKILTU*) (neut.) 'obligation' hence 'regulation; treaty'
ištanzan- (ZI-*(an)*-) (comm.) 'soul'
kā/ank-^{hhi} 'to hang' (trans.)
karpiya- 'to lift; perform, carry out' (alternate stem of *karp-*)
keššar- (ŠU, *QATU*) (comm.) 'hand' (§4.80)
^{TÚG}*kureššar* (neut.) 'scarf'
kūrur- 'hostility; hostile' (see §§4.85–4.86 and footnotes)
luzzi- (neut.) 'compulsory public work, corvée'
nēpiš- (AN, *ŠAMÊ*) (neut.) 'heaven, sky'
šā/ekk-^{hhi} (Akk. *IDI*) 'to know; recognize'
šarnikzil- (comm. and neut.) 'restitution'
šardi(y)a- (*NĀRĀRU*) (comm.) 'helper, auxiliary'
ši(p)pā/and- and (OH) *išpā/and-*^{hhi} (BAL) 'to libate'; plus *-kkan* 'to consecrate/sacrifice (acc.) to (dat.)[125]
takšūl- (neut.) 'peace'[126]
wāš-^{hhi} 'to buy'
waštūl- (neut.) 'sin'
zāḫ-/zaḫ(ḫ)-^{hhi} 'to strike' (+ *anda* 'to penetrate(?)')
ALAM (neut.) 'image, figurine' (probably *ēš(ša)ri-* but more than one word behind the Sumerogram is possible)
^{GIŠ}BANŠUR-*u-* (comm.) 'table'
GUD.NIGA (or GU_4.NIGA) (comm.) 'fattened ox'
LÚ ^{GIŠ}TUKUL (comm.) 'man having a TUKUL obligation'
MUNUS ŠU.GI (comm.) 'old woman, ritual practitioner'
NU.GÁL ' (there) is/are not'
ŠÀ (neut.) 'insides; womb'
^{d}UD.SIG_5 (comm.) 'the Favorable Day' (as a deity)

124. The force of *āppa* in this combination is 'back', referring to 'throwing back' the two parts of a door or window.

125. Reflecting that almost anything offered to deities was consecrated by pouring a libation over it.

126. As a predicate with 'to be', *takšul-* functions as an adjective 'peaceable'. Attributive use is very rare (see note 214 to §4.62 and cf. *kūrur-*).

Lesson 9

Grammar

This lesson introduces noun stems in *-āi-*, the nouns 'land, country' and 'heart', and *ḫi*-verbs with stems in *-i-*.

Noun stems in *-āi-* show either a fixed stem *-āi-* (written *-āy-* before vowels in broad transcription) or *-āi-* alternating with *-i(y)-*. Read §4.31 and memorize the paradigms for *lingāi-* 'oath' (comm.) (§4.32) and *ḫaštāi-* 'bone' (neut.) (§4.33). Learn the irregular paradigms of *utnē-* 'land' (§4.52) and *kart-* 'heart' (§4.120). Note that in NH the dative-locative singular of 'land' is identical to the nominative-accusative singular.

The *ḫi*-conjugation verbs with stems in *-i-* show a three-way stem alternation *-e-*, *-ai-* and *-i(y)-*. There is a tendency for the long diphthong variant *-āi* of the pres. 3 sg. to replace *-ai-* (cf. §11.17). Read §13.20 and memorize just the **present tense** portion of the paradigms for *dai-* 'put, place' and *pai-* 'give' (§13.21), as well as the unique paradigm of *nai-* (§13.23).

Translation Exercise

♦ 9.1. DUMU.É.GAL-*iš* ^{d}*Ḫa-an-ta-še-pa-an* LUGAL-*i*[127] *ki-iš-ša-ri-i da-a-i te-eš-šu-um-me-in-na pa-a-i*

9.2. DUMU.MEŠ É.GAL DINGIR-*LÌ-ni pé-ra-an ti-ya-an-zi*[128] *nu-uš-ši* NINDA-*an* ^{DUG}*iš-pa-an-tu-uz-zi-ya pé-ra-an kat-ta ti-an-zi*[128]

♦ 9.3. *nu ku-it-ma-an A-NA* ^{LÚ}SANGA *pa-a-an-zi ku-it-ma-an* ^{LÚ}SANGA ^{URU}*Aš-ta-ta-za ú-wa-da-an-zi ku-it-ma-an ú-wa-an-zi ŠA* DINGIR-*LÌ ša-ak-la-uš ta-ni-nu-wa-an-zi*[129]

♦ 9.4. DUMU.É.GAL LUGAL-*i pé-ra-an ḫu-wa-a-i na-aš ú-ez-zi*[130] DAM ^{LÚ}GUDU$_{12}$-*aš kat-ta*[131] *ti-i-e-ez-zi*

127. For the case of LUGAL-*i*, see §16.59 note 37.

128. Hittite scribes tended to spell the pres. 3 pl. of *tiya-* 'to step' as *ti-ya-an-zi* and that of *dai-* 'to put' as *ti-an-zi*, but this is not a reliable criterion, and you should assign these forms to the respective verbs based on the overall context.

129. This example is part of an oracular inquiry. Interpret the final clause as a question: 'Shall/should they. . . ?'.

130. See §24.31 for this as a pre-"serial" verb construction. The same applies to that in sentence 9.6. (cf. §24.32).

131. See vocabulary.

9.5. *šal-la-e-eš* DINGIR.MEŠ-*eš a-da-an-zi Ú-UL-ma-at-za iš-pí-ya-an-zi*

♦ 9.6. *ma-a-an-wa-ra-an*[132] *Ú-UL-ma e-ep-te-e-ni nu-wa-ra-an-mu pa-ra-a Ú-UL pé-eš-te-e-ni nu-wa ú-wa-mi nu-wa-aš-ma-aš QA-DU* KUR-*KU-NU ar-ḫa ḫar-ni-ik-mi*

♦ 9.7. [*le-e ku-i*]*š-ki*[133] *te-ez-zi* LUGAL-*ša*[134] *du-ud-du-mi-li kar-di-ya-aš-ša-aš*[135] [*i-e-ez-zi*]

◊ 9.8. *nu-za-an*[136] *ud-da-a-ar-me-et*[137] *ḫa-at-ta-ta-me-et-ta*[137] *kar-ta ša-it-ti*[138]

◊ 9.9. *ma-a-an-kán A-NA* ᵈUTU-*ŠI ku-iš-ki*[133] *pé-ra-an ar-ḫa wa-at-ku-zi na-aš-kán tu-uk*[139] *an-da ú-ez-zi e-ep-ti-ma-an Ú-UL na-an-mu pa-ra-a Ú-UL pé-eš-ti*[140]

◊9.10. *nu-uš-ši na-aš-šu* EGIR-*an ti-ya-ši na-aš-ma-an-kán* IGI.ḪI.A-*wa* ḪUR.SAG-*i na-it-ti nu-ut-ta NI-IŠ* DINGIR.MEŠ *pár-ḫe-eš-kán-zi*

◊ 9.11. *nu-uš-ša-an ke-e*[141] *ḫu-u-ma-an-ta* ᴳᴵŠ*pád-da-ni te-eḫ-ḫé* ᴳᴵŠ*pád-da-ra-aš-ša-an ḫa-aš-ši-i te-eḫ-ḫé*

♦9.12. *ma-a-an I-NA* UD.15.KAM ᵈ*SÎN-aš a-ki* KUR-*e an-da ma-ša-aš pa-ra-a-i* BURU$_{14}$ḪI.A *ka-ra-a-pí*[142]

♦9.13. UGULA LÚ ᴳᴵŠBANŠUR ᴳᴵŠBANŠUR ᴳᴵŠAB-*ya pé-ra-an da-a-i nu-uš-ša-an* 2 NINDA.GUR$_4$.RA.ḪI.A GAL 10 NINDA.GUR$_4$.RA TUR ᴳᴵŠBANŠUR-*i da-a-i*

♦9.14. *nu ḫa-aš-ta-a-e*[143] *an-da li-iš-ša-an-zi na-at ḫa-aš-ši-i a-wa-an kat-ta ti-an-zi*

♦9.15. *nu-kán ma-aḫ-ḫa-an* [ᵐ*Ar-nu-wa-a*]*n-da-aš* ᵐ*Zi-ta-aš-ša* KUR-*e kat-ta-an-da a-ra-an-zi*[144] [*nu* LÚ.KÚR-*aš*] *za-aḫ-ḫi-ya me-na-aḫ-ḫa-an-da*[145] *ú-ez-zi*

132. The reference is to a fugitive whose return is being demanded by the Hittite king.

133. *kuiški* is nom. sg. comm. of the indefinite pronoun 'anyone'. Here 'no one'.

134. The *-a* here is that which geminates the preceding consonant (§29.25), translatable here as 'Even the king . . .' (see §28.143).

135. *-šaš* is gen. sg. of the possessive enclitic adjective 'his'. For the syntax and meaning of *kardiyaš=šaš*, see §16.46.

136. Read either as *nu=z=(š)an* or *nu=z=an*, with the reflexive particle and one of the local particles *-(š)šan* or *-an* (see §28.19). For the use of *-(š)šan*, see §28.75.

137. *-met* is nom.-acc. neut. pl. of the possessive adjective 'my'. For *ḫattata* as specifically plural, see §1.145 and §4.106.

138. Substituted here for the original *ši-iš< -ša>-at-ti*, on which, see lesson 11.

139. *tuk* is dative-accusative of the accented personal pronoun 'you' (singular).

140. This entire sentence is a series of subordinate clauses. These are continued in sentence 10, where you will finally find the main clause.

141. *kē* is 'these' (nom.-acc. pl. neut.).

142. The absence of any conjunctions linking the successive clauses needs explanation. In texts such as the Laws and certain, originally OH, omen texts with *takku* followed by an apodosis, the apodosis (in our present case KUR-*e an-da*) regularly is asyndetic. For this as likely imitation of Akkadian, see §29.18, end.

143. The reference is to a sacrificial animal.

144. The reference here is to past time. For this use of the present tense, see §22.14 (the immediate context argues for "foregrounding" in this example.

145. The understood referent in context is 'them' (Arnuwanda and Zida). This is effectively a case of "pro-drop" with a postposition.

Broad Transcription

♦ 9.1. DUMU.É.GAL-*iš* ^{d}*Ḫantašepan* LUGAL-*i kiššarī dāi teššumminn≈a pāi*

9.2. DUMU.MEŠ É.GAL DINGIR-*LÌ-ni peran tiyanzi nu≈šši* NINDA-*an* ^{DUG}*išpantuzzi≈ya peran katta tianzi*

♦ 9.3. *nu kuitman ANA* ^{LÚ}SANGA *pānzi kuitman* ^{LÚ}SANGA ^{URU}*Aštataza uwadanzi kuitman uwanzi ŠA* DINGIR-*LÌ šaklauš taninuwanzi*

♦ 9.4. DUMU.É.GAL LUGAL-*i peran ḫuwāi n≈aš uezzi* DAM ^{LÚ}GUDU$_{12}$-*aš katta tiyēzzi*

9.5. *šallaēš* DINGIR.MEŠ-*eš adanzi ŪL≈ma≈at≈za išpiyanzi*

♦ 9.6. *mān≈war≈an ŪL≈ma ēptēni nu≈war≈an≈mu parā ŪL peštēni nu≈wa uwami nu≈wa≈šmaš QADU* KUR≈*KUNU arḫa ḫarnikmi*

♦ 9.7. *lē kuiški tezzi* LUGAL-*š≈a duddumili kardiyaš≈šaš iezzi*

◊ 9.8. *nu≈z≈(š*$^{?}$*)an uddār≈met ḫattata≈mett≈a karta šaitti*

♦ 9.9. *mān≈kan ANA* ^{d}UTU-*ŠI kuiški peran arḫa watkuzi n≈aš≈kan tuk anda uezzi ēpti≈ma≈an ŪL n≈an≈mu parā ŪL pešti*

◊9.10. *nu≈šši naššu* EGIR-*an tiyaši našma≈an≈kan* IGI.ḪI.A-*wa* ḪUR.SAG-*i naitti nu≈tta NIŠ* DINGIR.MEŠ *parḫeškanzi*

◊ 9.11. *nu≈ššan kē ḫūmanta* ^{GIŠ}*paddani teḫḫe* ^{GIŠ}*paddar≈a≈ššan ḫaššī teḫḫe*

♦9.12. *mān INA* UD.15.KAM ^{d}*SÎN-aš aki* KUR-*e anda mašaš parāi* BURU$_{14}$ḪI.A *karāpi*

9.13. UGULA LÚ ^{GIŠ}BANŠUR ^{GIŠ}BANŠUR ^{GIŠ}AB-*ya peran dāi nu≈ššan* 2 NINDA.GUR$_{4}$.RA.ḪI.A GAL 10 NINDA.GUR$_{4}$.RA TUR ^{GIŠ}BANŠUR-*i dāi*

♦9.14. *nu ḫaštāe šarā liššanzi n≈at ḫaššī awan katta tianzi*

♦9.15. *nu≈kan maḫḫan* ^{m}*Arnuwandaš* ^{m}*Zitašš≈a* KUR-*e kattanda aranzi nu* LÚ.KÚR-*aš zaḫḫiya menaḫḫanda uezzi*

Vocabulary

āppan (EGIR-*an*) 'behind, after' (*āppan tiya-* 'to step behind' = 'to support')
awan katta 'down beside'
^{d}*Ḫantašepa-* (comm.) (a minor deity, here referring to an image or symbol of the deity)
ḫaštāi- (neut.) 'bone'
ḫattātar (neut.) 'wise thought'[146]
ḫuwai-^{ḫḫi} 'to stir (intr.), to move (intr.), to proceed; to flee'[147]
išpai-^{ḫḫi} 'to be satisfied'
^{DUG}*išpantuzzi-* (neut.) 'libation-vessel'

146. For this meaning of *ḫattātar* (especially in the plural), see Hoffner 1998b: 66.

147. Against the *communis opinio*, there is no basis whatsoever for attributing a sense of haste to this verb. See correctly HW^{2} 3.805b. The Hittite verb for 'to run' is *piddai-*^{ḫḫi}.

karā/ep-^{ḫḫi} ‘to devour’
katta (GAM) (postpos., §20.27) ‘with, beside’ (not the same as *katta* ‘down’)
kattanda (GAM-*anda*) ‘down in(to)’
**kēr/kard(iy)-* (ŠÀ) (neut.) ‘heart’ (§4.120)
kuitman ‘while, as long as; until’
le/išš- ‘to gather, pick up’
luttāi- (^{GIŠ}AB) (neut.) ‘window’
maša- (comm.) ‘locust’
nai-^{ḫḫi} ‘to turn; send’
naššu . . . našma ‘either . . . or’
pai-^{ḫḫi} ‘to give’ (+ *parā* ‘to hand over, extradite’)
parā-^{ḫḫi} ‘to appear, come forth’
$^{\text{GI/GIŠ}}$*pattar* (neut.) ‘basket’
šai-^{ḫḫi} ‘to press; seal’ (but see §13.30!)
šakl(ā)i- (comm.) ‘custom, rule; prerogative, right; rite, ceremony (as the prerogative of a deity)[148]
dai-^{ḫḫi} ‘to put, place’
taninu- ‘to put in order, arrange’
utnē- (KUR) (neut.) ‘land, country’
uwate- ‘to bring’ (a person) (see §12.23)
watku- ‘to spring, jump’ (+ *peran arḫa* ‘to flee from’)
zaḫḫāi- (comm.) ‘battle’
BURU$_{14}$ = ‘crop(s), harvest; harvest-season’
DAM-*a-* (comm.) ‘wife’
^{LÚ}GUDU$_{12}$-*a-* (comm.) (A kind of priest, ranked below the ^{LÚ}SANGA/^{LÚ}*šankunni*-priests, but above other temple personnel such as exorcists (^{LÚ}AZU/^{LÚ}ḪAL), cooks, table-men, scribes and musicians. Its Hittite reading is most likely *kumra-* comm. with Hoffner 1996a.)
LÚ ^{GIŠ}BANŠUR (comm.) ‘table-man’ (server)
TUR ‘small, little’
UGULA (comm.) ‘chief, head’
QADU ‘(together) with’
^{d}*SÎN-a-* (comm.) ‘moon, Moon-god’ (= *arma-*)

148. For the meaning ‘prerogative’ and its role as the source of the meaning ‘rite (for a deity)’, see CHD Š 46 and Hoffner 2001.

Lesson 10

Grammar

This lesson introduces demonstrative/anaphoric, interrogative/relative and indefinite pronouns and *ḫi*-verbs with stems in *-a-*.

Read §§7.1–7.2 and memorize the paradigms of *apā-* 'that; he, she, it' and *kā-/kī-* 'this' (§7.3), ignoring as usual rare forms and footnotes—the distal demonstrative will be introduced in lesson 14. You have already seen some of the endings of these paradigms in the enclitic pronouns, but others are new and unique. For the syntax of the demonstratives, read carefully §§17.23–17.29. Further uses will be covered in footnotes.

The interrogative/relative pronoun *kui-* inflects as an ordinary *i*-stem in certain cases but like the demonstrative pronouns in others. Learn the regular forms of the paradigm in §8.2.

The indefinite pronoun *kuiški* 'some, any' adds a particle *-kki/-kka* to the inflected forms of *kui-* (see the paradigm in §8.3). Note that with rare exceptions the distribution of the variants *-kki/-kka* are governed by the last preceding vowel (*-kki* if the latter is an *i*, otherwise *-kka*). Similarly, *kuišša* 'each, every' consists of the inflected forms of *kui-* plus the conjunction geminating *-a/-ya* (see §8.3). One can only determine the difference between unitary 'each, every' and *kuiš* plus *-a/-ya* 'also who' from context, but the former should be assumed unless the context demands the latter.

Study §§17.53–17.56 on the syntax of indefinites, noting in particular that as subjects they often appear preverbally. Read §§27.5–27.9 for the syntax of interrogatives and §§30.97–30.104 regarding the syntax of the most frequent type of Hittite relative clause, which is quite different from that of English. You should also cursorily read §§30.83–30.96 to familiarize yourself with the many other relative clause structures in Hittite.

Most *ḫi*-verbs in *-a-* show a fixed stem *-a-* except for the first person plural, infinitive and verbal noun, which show a stem in *-um-*. Read §13.18 with references and memorize just the **present tense** portions of the paradigms of *dā-* 'take' (§13.16) and *tarna-* 'release' in §13.18). Note that there is a tendency to level out the forms in *-um-*, especially in *dā-* 'to take'.

Translation Exercise

♦ 10.1. *nu A-BU-ŠU ku-e-el wa-aš-ta-i kat-ta-ma*[149] DUMU-*ŠU Ú-UL wa-aš-du-la-aš-pát*[150] *nu-uš-ši-kán* É *A-BI-ŠU ar-ḫa da-an-zi*

♦ 10.2. *ták-ku* ÌR-*aš ḫu-wa-a-i na-aš A-NA* KUR *Lu-ú-i-ya pa-iz-zi ku-i-ša-an a-ap-pa ú-wa-te-ez-zi nu-uš-še*[151] 6 GÍN KÙ.BABBAR *pa-a-i*

♦ 10.3. ^{d}IŠKUR-*aš* ^{d}NIN.TU-*ni te-e-et ma-a-aḫ-ḫa-an*[152] *i-ya-u-e-ni ki-iš-ta-an-ti-it ḫar-ku-e-ni*

♦ 10.4. GUD *pu-u-ḫu-ga-ri-in-ma ku-e-da-ni* UD-*ti ú-nu-e-er nu-za* ^{d}UTU-*ŠI a-pé-e-da-ni* UD-*ti wa-ar-ap-ta*

♦ 10.5. *nu ma-aḫ-ḫa-an* MU.KAM-*za me-ḫur ti-ya-zi*[153] *še-li-aš šu-un-nu-ma-an-zi nu-kán BI-IB-RU ŠA* ^{d}LIŠ ^{URU}*Ša-mu-ḫa* ^{URU}*Ḫa-at-tu-ša-za kat-ta ú-da-an-zi*

♦ 10.6. *nu* ^{DUG}*ḫar-ši-ya-al-li ḫé-e-ša-an-zi*[154] *še-li-uš-ma šu-un-na-an-zi nu-kán* ^{DUG}*ḫar-ši-ya-al-li ḫal-ki-ya-aš-ša*[155] *šu-un-na-an-zi ŠA* GEŠTIN-*ya-kán šu-un-na-an-zi*

♦ 10.7. ÌR-*YA-ma-wa nu-u-ma-an da-aḫ-ḫi nu-wa-ra-an-za-an*[156] ^{LÚ}*MU-TI*$_4$*-YA i-ya-mi*

◊ 10.8. *ku-iš-ma-kán*[157] *ke-e-el tup-pí-aš* 1-*an-na*[158] *me-mi-an wa-aḫ-nu-zi na-an-kán ku-u-uš*[159] *li-in-ki-ya-aš* DINGIR.MEŠ-*eš ar-ḫa ḫar-ni-in-kán-zi*

◊ 10.9. *ku-it*[160]*-wa-ra-aš*[161] *ú-ez-zi* AN-*aš* ^{d}UTU-*uš*[161] KUR-*e-aš* ^{LÚ}SIPA.UDU-*aš ú-ez-zi-ma*[162]*-wa-ra-aš ku-e-da-ni me-mi-ya-ni*

♦ 10.10. *ki-i-wa ku-it Ú-UL-wa*[163] *ŠA* MUNUS TÚG.NÍG.LÁM.MEŠ

♦ 10.11. *ták-ku* LÚ-*aš EL-LU*$_4$ *ḫal-ki-aš* ÉSAG-*an ta-a-i-ez-zi* ÉSAG-*ša ḫal-ki-in ú-e-mi-ez-zi* ÉSAG-*an ḫal-ki-it šu-un-na-i Ù* 12 GÍN KÙ.BABBAR *pa-a-i*

149. The meaning of *katta=ma* in this context is 'consequently'.

150. Interpret this clause as a (rhetorical) question. See §§26.7–26.9. The following clause continues the rhetorical question, and the force of the negative carries over, as in English (§26.23)—likewise in sentence 10.7. For the meaning of the genitive *waštulaš*, see §16.46. Likewise GEŠTIN-*aš* in sentence 10.6. The force of the *-pat* in this case is 'likewise, too'.

151. The form *-šše* instead of usual *-šši* for enclitic dat. sg. 'him, her' appears only in Old Hittite.

152. Interpret *māḫḫan* here as interrogative. Idiomatic English prefers 'what?' instead of 'how?'.

153. MU.KAM-*za me-ḫur* shows an adverbial accusative (see §16.7 note 4).

154. Sentence 6 directly continues sentence 5.

155. For the word order, cf. the last example in §16.36. The "genitive of material" has variable word order vis-à-vis its head noun.

156. In NH the enclitic accusative pronoun is sometimes repeated, framing either *-z*(*a*) or one of the dat./acc. personal pronouns. See §30.21, end.

157. Since *waḫnu-* here has the meaning 'to alter, change', it takes telicizing *-kkan* (see §28.114).

158. The geminating *-a* here is the additive focus particle, in this case meaning 'even' (see §28.143).

159. As elsewhere in Neo-Hittite, *kūš* is functioning here as common gender *nominative* plural.

160. *kuit* 'what?' here has the meaning 'why?'. See §8.9.

161. For the syntax of this sentence, see §30.41.

162. For the "anaphoric" use of *-ma*, see §§28.151 and 30.29. Here, as often, mere change of topic is enough to induce the use of *-a/-ma*.

163. Hittite does not always require a subject clitic pronoun when the antecedent is clear from the context (§17.21). The trace after *-wa* on the tablet shows that the scribe, finding himself running out of space on the line, at first started to write *-wa-ra-at* but stopped and erased the *-ra*, apparently deciding that the reference was clear without it.

♦10.12. *ḫa-a-aš*[164] *nu-wa ku-e-ez ú-wa-ši šu-up-pa-az-wa ú-wa-mi nu-wa ku-e-ez šu-up-pa-ya-az*[165] . . . ^{d}UTU-*wa-aš-wa* É-*az*[165] *nu-wa ku-e-ez* ^{d}UTU-*az*[165]

♦10.13. $^{\mathrm{f.d}}$*IŠTAR-at-ti-iš ku-wa-at-ta im-ma ku-wa-at-ta še-er* TUKU.TUKU-*u-an-za na-an a-ri-ya-u-e-ni*

◊10.14. *ku-iš-ma ke-e-da-ni* KUR-*e A-NA* $^{\mathrm{m.d}}$LAMMA *ú-wa-a-i*[166] *pé-e-da-i . . . na-aš-ma-aš-ši pí-ya-an ku-it ḫar-mi nu-uš-ši-kán*[167] *ar-ḫa ku-it-ki da-a-i . . . na-an-kán ku-u-uš*[159] *NI-IŠ* DINGIR.MEŠ *ar-ḫa ḫar-ni-in-kán-zi*

♦10.15. MUNUS.LUGAL ^{f}*Pu-du-ḫé-pa-aš-kán ku-wa-pí* ^{m}UR.MAḪ.LÚ-*in* GAL DUB.SAR.MEŠ ^{URU}*Ḫa-at-tu-ši A-NA ṬUPPA*$^{\mathrm{ḪI.A}}$ ^{URU}*Ki-iz-zu-wa-at-na ša-an-ḫu-u-wa-an-zi ú-e-ri-ya-at na-aš-ta*[168] *ke-e ṬUPPA*$^{\mathrm{ḪI.A}}$ *ŠA* EZEN$_4$ *ḫi-šu-wa-a-aš a-pí-ya* UD-*at*[169] *ar-ḫa a-ni-ya-at*

Vocabulary

aniya- 'to carry out, execute; write'
ariya- 'to make (the subject of) an oracular inquiry'
^{d}*Ḫannaḫanna-* (^{d}NIN.TU) (comm.) (fate-goddess)
^{DUG}*ḫaršiyalli-* (neut.) 'pithos, storage jar'
EZEN$_4$ *ḫišuwa-* (a major festival; the Hittite noun underlying the logogram EZEN$_4$ is comm. gender)
kištant- (comm.) 'hunger'
kuwapi 'where; (NH only) when'
kuwatta šer 'on what account, why'
lingāi- (comm.) 'oath'
nūman (marks negative volition of subject; see §26.17) translatable as 'do/did not wish to . . .'
pēda-^{ḫḫi} 'to carry (off)'[170]
GUD *pūḫugari-* (comm.) 'ox of ritual substitution'
šēli- (comm.) 'grain-heap, granary'
šunna-^{ḫḫi} 'to fill'
dā-^{ḫḫi} 'to take' (+*parā* 'to pick out')
uda-^{ḫḫi} 'to bring'
waḫnu- 'to turn (usually tr.); change, alter'

164. This Hittite version of "twenty questions" begins with a brusque demand: 'open (up)!'. One should take *šuppa(ya)z* as elliptical for 'holy place'. The use of *nu* in the responses instead of the usual asyndeton implies a suitably impolite retort: 'so'. Cf. §29.48.

165. See §30.44 for this instance of "gapping."

166. For the spelling of this word, see note 185 to §1.123.

167. The *-kkan* is required by the preverb *arḫa* and the separation from the person implied by it (see §28.113 and §16.60).

168. The particle *-ašta* combined with *arḫa* underscores that the new tablets were copied *from* the old ones.

169. *apiya* UD-*at* (= *šiwat*) is an archaic expression for *apēdani* UD-*ti*.

170. But Hittite speakers can manipulate the "deictic center," and the force of *pēda-* and *uda-* must be determined by context, just like English 'bring' and 'take' for speakers for whom these are directional.

wāi- (neut.) 'woe'[171]
warp- 'to bathe'
wašta-$^{\textit{ḫḫi}}$ 'to sin'
wēštara- (^{LÚ}SIPA-*a-*) (comm.) 'shepherd'
ÉSAG-*(n)a-* (comm.) 'grain storage pit'
GAL DUB.SAR.MEŠ 'chief of the scribes'
GÍN 'shekel'
^{d}LIŠ (comm.) '(the goddess) Ishtar' (this goddess's name is also written ^{d}*IŠTAR*, and in the woman's name $^{f.d}$*IŠTAR-at-ti-iš* [= $^{f.d}$*Šaušgattiš*] is read as ^{d}*Šaušga*)
TÚG.NÍG.LÁM.MEŠ 'festive garments'
BIBRU 'rhyton, animal-shaped drinking vessel'
ELLU 'free'
$^{f.d}$*IŠTAR-at-ti-iš*, see above under ^{d}LIŠ
^{LÚ}*MUTU* (comm.) 'husband'
ṬUPPU (neut.) 'clay tablet'

171. This NH word is a loanword from Luwian *wāyit-*. Old Hittite has a native equivalent *wāi-* that is common gender.

Lesson 11

Grammar

This lesson introduces enclitic possessive pronouns, accented personal pronouns, vocatives and *ḫi*-verbs with alternating stems in *-a-/-i-* (including the suffix *-anna/i-*) and with the suffix *-šša-*.

In Old and Middle Hittite possessive pronouns usually appear as inflected enclitics attached to their head noun. Except in rare cases, possession is indicated in NH by the genitive of the accented personal pronouns or by dative enclitic pronouns. Read chapter 6 in its entirety, with close attention to how pronouns express possession at different stages of the language. Memorize the paradigms of enclitic possessives in §6.4. Note the special "split possessive" construction that is used particularly with inalienably possessed nouns (§§16.31–16.33).

Accented pronouns for the first and second person are used for emphasis or contrast. Their inflection is limited and quite irregular. Read §5.6 and memorize the paradigms in §5.7. Note that in NH the dative-accusative forms of the first person singular and plural and second person plural come to be used also for the nominative. The demonstrative stem *apā-* also functions as the accented pronoun for the third person. See §§17.2–17.4 on the syntax of the accented personal pronouns, including *apā-*.

True vocatives are relatively rare and limited to Old and Middle Hittite. See §§3.18–3.20 for the attested forms. Less common but attested in several cases is "appositional direct address."

Some *ḫi*-verbs are inflected consistently with *-a-* in the singular but in the plural may show either *-i(y)-* or *-a-* (the *-i(y)-* forms occur mostly in older texts). Memorize the **present tense** portion of the paradigm for *mema/i-* in §13.25. Verbs with the suffix *-anna/i-* show the same inflection (read §13.27 and study the examples in §13.28). The verbs *unna/i-* and *penna/i-* 'drive' inflect partly like *mema/i-* and partly like *tarna-*, showing some forms in *-um-* (see §13.18). Derived verbs in *-šša-* inflect with invariant *-a-*. Study the examples in §13.14, noting the irregular archaic variants of *ī/ēšš(a)-*. The suffixes *-šša-* and *-anna/i-* have the same range of pluractional meanings as stems in *-ške-* introduced in lesson 6. See again the gist of §§24.9–24.20.

Translation Exercise

11.1. ^{d}UTU-*i iš-ḫa-a-mi ku-it-wa wa-aš-túl-me-et ku-it-wa i-ya-nu-un ku-it*[172]

11.2. ^{LÚ}SIPA-*aš* GUD.ḪI.A-*šu-uš* UDU.ḪI.A-*šu-uš ne-ku-uz me-e-ḫur a-ša-u-ni a-ap-pa pé-en-na-i*

11.3. ^{d}UTU-*e šar-ku* LUGAL-*u-e ta-an-du-ke-eš-na-aš* DUMU.MEŠ-*aš* ^{LÚ}SIPA-*aš zi-ik*[173] *nu* DINGIR.MEŠ-*na-aš iš-tar-na la-a-ma-an-te-et na-ak-ki-i*[174] *nu* KUR.KUR.MEŠ *ḫu-u-ma-an-te-eš tu-uk-pát šar-li-iš-kán-zi*

♦ 11.4. *zi-ik am-me-el* É-*na le-e ú-wa-ši ú-ga*[175] *tu-e-el pár-na Ú-UL ú-wa-a-mi*

◊ 11.5. *nam-ma-za* DINGIR.MEŠ *me-ḫu-na-aš*[176] *e-eš-ša-an-zi ku-e-da-ni-ya*[177] DINGIR-*LÌ-ni ku-it me-ḫur na-an a-pé-e-da-ni me-ḫu-ni e-eš-ša-an-zi*

♦ 11.6. *ma-aḫ-ḫa-an-ma A-BU-YA* ŠEŠ-*YA ku-in* ^{LÚ}*tu-u-ḫu-kán-ta-ḫi-ti ti-ya-an ḫar-ta na-an ar-ḫa ti-it-ta-nu-ut*[178] *nu am-mu-uk* LUGAL-*ez-na-an-ni ti-it-ta-nu-ut*

♦ 11.7. *ták-ku* ÌR-*na-aš na-aš-ma* GÉME-*aš QA-AS-SÚ na-aš-ma* GÌR=*ŠU ku-iš-ki tu-wa-ar-ni-iz-zi* 10 GÍN KÙ.BABBAR *pa-a-i*

♦ 11.8. *ták-ku* LÚ.U$_{19}$.LU-*an EL-LA*$_{12}$[179] KIR$_4$-*še-et*[179] *ku-iš-ki wa-a-ki* 1 MA.NA KÙ.BABBAR *pa-a-i*

♦ 11.9. *zi-ga-az* ^{GIŠ}*ḫa-tal-ki-iš-na-aš*[180] *ḫa-me-eš-ḫi-ya-az*[181] BABBAR-*TÌ wa-aš-ša-ši* BURU$_{14}$-*ma-az iš-ḫar-wa-an-da*[182] *wa-aš-ša-ši*

◊ 11.10. *nu ma-a-an A-NA* KUR ^{URU}*Ḫa-at-ti pár-ḫu-wa-an-zi ú-wa-at-te-ni nu-uš-ma-aš-kán* ^{d}ZA.BA$_4$.BA$_4$-*aš* ^{GIŠ}TUKUL.ḪI.A-*KU-NU a-ap-pa na-a-i nu šu-me-en-za-an-pát* ^{UZU}Ì *e-ez-za-az-zi*

◊ 11.11. ^{LÚ}*me-ne-ya-aš ke-e-et-ta ke-e-et-ta*[183] GI-*an ḫu-ut-ti-an-na-i*[184] *tar-na-a-i-ma-an na-at-ta i-i*[185] *ḫal-zi-iš-ša-i*

◊ 11.12. *A-NA* ^{d}IŠKUR ^{URU}*Ne-ri-ik ku-it* SÍSKUR *up-pí-u-e-ni na-at* KASKAL-*ši le-e ku-iš-ki wa-al-aḫ-zi*

172. The repetition of the pronoun *kuit* in the second clause shows a certain impatience or urgency, perhaps like English 'what in the world...?' or 'whatever...?'.

173. For the word order of this clause, see §30.9.

174. On the possible interpretation of *nakkī* as a superlative 'most exalted', see §18.16.

175. The contrastive focus *-a* here, which does not geminate the preceding consonant (*-a/-ma*), underscores the change of subject: 'while I (for my part) ...'. See §28.155, end.

176. *meḫur* here has the meaning 'proper time'.

177. Interpret *kuedaniya* as a single word 'each'. See §8.3.

178. The syntax here is complex and unusual. One might have expected instead: ŠEŠ=*YA*=*ma kuin ABU*=*YA* ^{LÚ}*tūḫukantaḫiti tiyan ḫarta maḫḫan*=*ma*=*an arḫa tittanut* ...

179. For the syntax of this NS version, see §16.19. Cf. the older syntax of sentence 7!

180. For this common gender *a*-stem variant of 'hawthorn' and the motivation for it in this context, see §3.11.

181. Since the conjunction *-ya* 'also, and' makes no sense in this context, we must understand *ḫamešḫiya* as d.-l. singular, as if from an *i*-stem. See §3.28.

182. Nom.-acc. pl. neut. of the adjective used adverbially. See §19.3.

183. *kēt kētt*=*a* is the Old Hittite expression for 'on both this side and that'.

184. The stem form *ḫuttiya-* instead of *ḫuittiya-* is limited to Old Hittite. This refers to drawing an arrow back against the taut string of a bow prior to shooting. Note the iterative function of the pluractional suffix, probably matched by that in *ḫalziššai*.

185. Mimicking the cry of the bird or animal hunted. See §2.59.

♦11.13. *a-du-e-ni a-ku-e-ni nu* ^{URU}*Ḫa-at-tu-ša i-ya-an-na-aḫ-ḫé*[186] LUGAL-*ša* ^{URU}*A-ri-in-na pa-iz-zi*

♦11.14. NAM.RA.ḪI.A-*wa me-ek-ki*[187] *ú-e-da-u-e-ni* GUD.ḪI.A-*wa* UDU.ḪI.A ANŠE.KUR.RA.ḪI.A ANŠE.GÌR.NUN.NA.ḪI.A ANŠE.MEŠ *me-ek-ki*[187] *na-an-ni-ya-u-e-ni*

♦11.15. *ták-ku* GUD.ḪI.A A.ŠÀ-*ni pa-a-an-zi Ù*[188] *BE-EL* A.ŠÀ *ú-e-mi-<ez->zi* UD.1.KAM[189] *tu-u-ri-ez-zi ma-a-na-aš-ta*[190] MUL.ḪI.A-*eš ú-en-zi nu-uš a-ap-pa iš-ḫi-iš-ši pé-en-na-i*

Vocabulary

e/išḫarwant- 'bloody; blood-red'
ḫalziššа-^{ḫḫi} (pluractional stem to *ḫalzai-*^{ḫḫi} 'to call')
ḫamešḫa- (comm.) 'spring'
ḫatalkiš(n)- (neut.) 'hawthorn' (§4.89)
ḫuett(iya)- 'to draw (a bow)'
īšš(a)-/ēšš(a)-^{ḫḫi} (pluractional stem to *iya-* 'to do, make') (§13.14)
iyanna/i-^{ḫḫi} 'to set out; begin to move; go' (pluractional stem to m.-p. *iya-* 'to walk' introduced in lesson 13)
^{LÚ}*mene(y)a-* (comm.) (a cult functionary)
nanna/i-^{ḫḫi} 'to drive'
nāta- (GI) (comm.) 'reed; arrow'
palša- (KASKAL-*(š)a-*) (comm.) 'path, way; time, instance'
parḫ- 'to attack'
penna/i-^{ḫḫi} 'to drive (away)'
dandukiš(n)- (neut.) 'mortality' (§4.89); *dandukišnaš* DUMU-*(l)a-* 'child of mortality' = 'human being' (also written DUMU.NAM.LÚ.U_{19}.LU-*(l)a-*).
tarna-^{ḫḫi} 'to release, let go'
tit(ta)nu- 'to install' (+ *arḫa* 'to remove [from a position]')
^{LÚ}*tūḫukantaḫit-* (neut.) 'position of crown-prince' (see §§2.17 and 4.15)
tūriya- 'to hitch/yoke up'
d/tuwarni- 'to break' (in OH a *mi*-verb, in NH mostly replaced by *ḫi*-inflection; see paradigm in §12.26)
uppa/i-^{ḫḫi} 'to send'
wāk-^{ḫḫi} 'to bite'
wašše/a- 'to put on' (clothing) (+ *-za* = on oneself) (§12.21)
wi/edā(i)- 'to bring' (see note 118 to §12.23)

186. The ending *-ḫḫe* beside *-ḫḫi* is a feature of Old Hittite.

187. Since 'deportees', 'cattle' and 'sheep' are common gender even as collectives, this OH/NS example shows the original appositional syntax of *mekk(i)-*: 'a lot (of them)' (§18.10).

188. The presence of the Akkadian conjunction *U* (standing for *-a/-ma*, here marking a change of subject; cf. §28.155, end) marks the continuation of the protasis, while the absence of any conjunction preceding the third clause marks it as a main clause. See §§29.18, end, and 29.55.

189. Interpret UD.1.KAM as an 'accusative of extent' with a cardinal number. See §§9.41 and 16.24.

190. The particle *-ašta* in combination with the verb gives the force 'come *out*, appear'. The stars have passed from one defined space into another. See §28.69.

ANŠE-*a/i*- (comm.) 'ass, donkey'
ANŠE.GÌR.NUN.NA-*a*- (comm.) 'mule'
BURU$_{14}$ 'harvest; harvest season'
GÉME-*a*-[191] (comm.) 'female slave' (for the stem as *GÉME-*a/iššara*-, see LH 186 and note 28 to §2.39 in this grammar)
KIR$_4$ (neut.) 'nose'
LUGAL-*(u)eznātar* (neut.) 'kingship' (= **ḫaššuweznatar*)
MA.NA 'mina'
MUL (= *ḫašter*-) (comm.) 'star' (see §4.84)
NAM.RA-*a*- = *arnuwala*- (comm.) 'deportee'; i.e., foreign civilian seized by the Hittites and forcibly resettled elsewhere)
ŠEŠ-*(n)a*- (*negna*-) (comm.) 'brother'
^{GIŠ}TUKUL-*(l)i*- (comm.)[192] 'weapon'
^{UZU}Ì 'flesh; fat' (*šākan*-) (neut.)
^{d}ZA.BA$_4$.BA$_4$-*a*- (comm.) (a wargod)
QASSU 'his/her hand' (< *QAT* + -*ŠU*, §32.18)

191. The Hittite word for 'female slave' is the word for 'male slave' + the female-indicating suffix -*(š)šara*- (LH 186).

192. On the gender of ^{GIŠ}TUKUL, see LH 48 n 147 (with contribution by Melchert). The nom.-acc. ^{GIŠ}TUKUL-*(l)i* forms are collectives. For the sense in the Laws (likely not 'weapon'), cf. Beal 1988.

Lesson 12

Grammar

This lesson introduces the preterite of the *ḫi*-conjugation, all remaining verbal classes and the irregular paradigm of *tamai-* 'other.'

Memorize the endings of the *ḫi*-conjugation preterite (§§11.5) and then review the **preterite portion** of the paradigms for all the classes of *ḫi*-verbs introduced: *šakk-* (§13.1), *šipand-* (§13.3), *dai-* and *pai-* (§13.21), *dā-* (§13.16), *tarna-* (§13.18), *mema/i-* and *ūnna/i-* (§13.25) and stems in *-anna/i-* (§13.28) and *-šša-* (§13.14). Read §§11.20–11.21 on the spread of the endings *-ta* and *-šta*, but you need not memorize the details, just be prepared to meet these in verbs where the original ending was *-(V)š*.

Derived verbs in *-aḫḫ-* are inflected as *ḫi*-verbs in Old Hittite but later migrate to the *mi*-conjugation. Either set of endings can be encountered, as shown in the paradigms in §13.8. A few monosyllabic stems in *-āi-* show a mixture of *mi-* and *ḫi*-endings. Learn the paradigms of *lāi-* and *ḫāi-* (§12.39).

The adjective *tamāi-* 'other' inflects as a stem *tamāi-* in the nominative and accusative and like a demonstrative pronoun in the rest of the paradigm: memorize the paradigm in §8.10. Read about its syntax in §§17.61–62.

Translation Exercise

◊ 12.1. *nu-ut-ták-kán* É *A-BI-KA* KUR-*KA-ya* *Ú-UL* *ar-ḫa da-aḫ-ḫu-un na-at da-me-e-da-ni ku-e-da-ni-ik-ki* *Ú-UL* *pé-eḫ-ḫu-un* *A-NA* KUR-*TI-ma ta-ma-a-in ku-in-ki* EN-*an* *Ú-UL* *i-ya-nu-un*

♦ 12.2. *nu-mu* NAM.RA *ku-in pa-ra-a pí-i-e-er na-aš* 4 *LI-IM* NAM.RA *e-eš-ta na-an-kán* URUKÙ.BABBAR-*ši* *pa-ra-a ne-eḫ-ḫu-un na-an ar-ḫa ú-wa-te-er*[193]

♦ 12.3. d*IŠTAR-ma-mu* GAŠAN-*YA* Ù-*at nu-mu* Ù-*it ki-i me-mi-iš-ta* DINGIR-*LÌ-ni-wa-at-ta am-mu-uk*[194] *tar-na-aḫ-ḫi nu-wa le-e na-aḫ-ti*

◊ 12.4. d*IŠTAR-ma-mu ḫu-wa-ap-pí* DINGIR-*LÌ-ni ḫu-wa-ap-pí* DI-*eš-ni pa-ra-a* *Ú-UL* *ku-wa-pí-ik-ki tar-na-aš*

193. Here NAM.RA = *arnuwala-* 'deportees' is treated as a collective singular, and the number and gender agreement is strictly grammatical. One must translate into idiomatic English with plurals.

194. In this NH text *ammuk* is functioning as a *nominative*.

♦ 12.5. *ka-ru-ú* ᵐ*U-uḫ-na-aš* LUGAL ᵁᴿᵁ*Za-a-al-pu-wa* ᵈ*ši-ú-šum-m*[*i-in*][195] [ᵁᴿ] ᵁ*Ne-e-ša-az* ᵁᴿᵁ*Za-a-al-pu-wa pé-e-d*[*a-aš ap-pé*]*-ez-zi-ya-na* ᵐ*A-ni-it-ta-aš* LUGAL.GAL[196] ᵈ*ši-ú-šu*[*m-*(*mi-in* ᵁ⁾ᴿᵁ*Z*]*a-a-al-pu-wa-az a-ap-pa* ᵁᴿᵁ*Ne-e-ša pé-e-*[*da-aḫ-ḫu-un*]

♦ 12.6. *BE-LÍ-NI-wa-an-na-aš ŠA* ᵁᴿᵁ*A-ri-ip-ša-a i-wa-ar* ᵁᴿᵁ*Ḫa-at-tu-ši ša-a-ru-wa-u-wa-an-zi le-e ma-ni-ya-aḫ-ti*[197]

♦ 12.7. *ták-ku* LÚ.U$_{19}$.LU*-an EL-LA-AM ku-iš-ki da-šu-wa-aḫ-ḫi na-aš-ma* ZU$_{9}$*ŠU la-a-ki ka-ru-ú* 1 MA.NA KÙ.BABBAR *pí-iš-ker ki-nu-na* 20 GÍN KÙ.BABBAR *pa-a-i*

♦ 12.8. *nu* ᵁᴿᵁ*Ne-e-ša-an iš-pa-an-di na-ak-ki-it*[198] *da-a-aš* ᵁᴿᵁ*Ne-e-ša-aš* LUGAL*-un IṢ-BAT Ù* DUMU.MEŠ[199] ᵁᴿᵁ*Ne-e-ša i-da-a-lu na-at-ta ku-e-da-ni-ik-ki ták-ki-iš-ta*

♦ 12.9. *nu ke-e* KUR.KUR.MEŠ *ḫar-ni-in-ku-un a-aš-šu-ma-aš-ši*[200] *ša-ra-a da-aḫ-ḫu-un nu* É*-er-mi-it a-aš-ša-u-i-it ša-ra-a šu-un-na-aḫ-ḫu-un*

♦12.10. *nam-ma-aš-ma-aš-kán* ÉRIN.MEŠ *iš-ḫe-eḫ-ḫu-un nu-mu* ÉRIN.MEŠ *pí-iš-ke-u-an*[201] *da-a-er na-at-mu la-aḫ-ḫi kat-ta-an pa-iš-ga-u-wa-an*[201] *ti-i-e-er*

♦ 12.11. *up-pé-eš-šar*ᴹᴱŠ*-ma-at-ta ku-e up-pa-aḫ-ḫu-un nu ḫu-u-ma-an*[202] *A-NA* LÚ *ṬE$_4$-ME-KA ma-ni-ya-aḫ-ḫu-un*

♦12.12. *ki-nu-na* ᵈUTU*-ŠI tu-uk* ᵐ*Ku-pa-an-ta-*ᵈLAMMA*-an Ú-UL ku-it-ki*[203] *i-da-la-u-wa-aḫ-ḫu-un*

♦12.13. *nu* ᵁᴿᵁ*Ne-ri-iq-qa-aš ku-it IŠ-TU* UD*-UM* ᵐ*Ḫa-an-ti-li ar-ḫa ḫar-ga-an-za e-eš-ta na-an* EGIR*-pa ú-e-da-aḫ-ḫu-un*[204]

◊12.14. ᵈ10 EN AN KI LUGAL DINGIR.MEŠ *ḫal-zi-ya-u-en nu-uš-ši ḫa-ra-a-tar wa-aš-túl-la pé-ra-an tar-nu-me-ni nu ŠA* ᵈ10 TUKU.TUKU*-an pé-ra-an la-a-u-e-ni*[205]

♦12.15. *nu-kán A-BU-YA ku-e-da-aš A-NA* URU.DIDLI.ḪI.A *da-an-na-at-ta-aš* EGIR*-an* AN.ZA.GÀR *ú-e-te-et na-aš* ᴸᵁKÚR *da-a-an nam-ma ḫar-ni-ik-ta*

195. Read as *šiun⸗šummin* with assimilation of the final *-n* of the noun. See §6.4 with note 11 on the meaning of the enclitic possessive *-šummi-*! The word ᵈ*šiu-* is an appellative meaning 'god', not a name.

196. This nominative phrase is in apposition to the first-person subject contained in the verb.

197. Context shows that *⸗nnaš* is the direct object of both the finite verb and the infinitive and ᵁᴿᵁ*Ḫattuši* is a recipient, not the (grammatically possible) direct object of the infinitive.

198. One must assume ellipsis here of a noun 'force', 'assault', or the like. Cf. CHD under *nakki-*². The context suggests a sense 'with a heavy force/assault' = 'with might, by storm'.

199. In the absence of any compelling examples of "partitive apposition" in the dative-locative with an indefinite one must take this as the regular partitive genitive (§16.35) with omission of *ŠA*. For the syntax of noun plus *natta kuedanikki*, see §26.6, last example.

200. It is uncertain whether the use of dat. sg. *-šši* to refer back to a *neuter* plural antecedent reflects regular OH grammar or an error by the copyist. The spelling of the enclitic possessive pronoun as *-mit* for the nom.-acc. sg. neut. *-met* is definitely an error (cf. §6.6).

201. For the syntax of these forms in *-wan*, read §§25.33–25.35.

202. This agreement pattern, by which a neuter singular 'everything' resumes a plural not referring to persons, is not unusual cross-clausally. Cf. §15.15.

203. *ŪL kuitki* is nom.-acc. sg. neuter functioning adverbially: 'in no way, not at all'.

204. The ablatival time expression forces a "state passive" reading of the predicate, not an analytic past perfect. For the inflection of *wedaḫḫun*, see the ref. in the vocabulary entry.

205. The verb *tarna-* in this context means 'to admit, confess'. The force of *-šši* carries over from the first sentence to the second, where one should also understand (*nu*)*⸗šši . . . peran*.

Vocabulary

appezzian 'afterwards' (nom.-acc. sg.neuter of *appezziya-* used adverbially)
ḫalzai-^{ḫḫi} 'to call, summon'
ḫarātar (neut.) 'offense'
ḫark- (+ *arḫa*) 'perish utterly, be destroyed'
išḫai-^{ḫḫi} 'to bind, tie; impose' (see §13.21)
idālawaḫḫ- 'to mistreat, harm'
kaka- (ZU$_{19}$) (comm.) 'tooth'
karū 'earlier, formerly; already' (see §19.11 with note 4)
kattan 'with, beside' (postposition, variant of *katta*, not the same as *kattan* 'below'!)
kinun 'now'
kuwapikki 'anywhere; any time'
lāḫḫa- (comm.) 'campaign; trip'
lāi- 'to release, let go, dispel'
lāk-^{ḫḫi} 'to knock down/out'
maniyaḫḫ- 'to hand over, assign, distribute, entrust; administer, govern'
mema/i-^{ḫḫi} 'to speak'
naḫ(ḫ)-^{ḫḫi} 'to be afraid' (construed both with nom. and non-nom. subject; cf. §30.13)
tak(ki)šš- 'to put together, make, perpetrate; wield' (§12.14)
dān 'a second time' *dān namma* 'again a second time' (cf. entry *namma* in lesson 2)
dannatta- 'empty, desolate'
dašuwaḫḫ- 'to blind'
uppeššar (neut.) 'thing sent, gift'
wete-/weda-^{ḫḫi} 'to build' (see §12.23 with note 118)
zašḫāi- (Ù) (comm.) 'dream'
zašḫiya- (Ù) 'to appear in a dream'
AN.ZA.GÀR 'tower'
DIDLI.ḪI.A (plural marker) (used exclusively with Sumerograms)
LÚ *ṬĒME* 'messenger' (= Akkad. *amēl ṭēme;* the LÚ is not a determinative)
IṢBAT 'took, seized' (= *ēpta*)
LĪM 'thousand'
-NI 'our' (used only after Sumerograms and Akkadian words)

Lesson 13

Grammar

This lesson introduces the medio-passive and the highly irregular verb *au(š)-* 'see.'

Memorize the paradigm of *au(š)-* §13.32. Note the mixture of *mi-* and *ḫi-*endings and the presence/absence of the *-š-*. The less common verb *mau(šš)-* 'fall' is inflected in the same way.

Read §§11.24–11.26 on the medio-passive endings and changes in them from OH to NH. Familiarize yourself with §§14.1–14.6 and the sample paradigms for consonantal stems (§14.2) and vocalic stems (§14.4). Verbs that take endings in the third person singular without *-tt-* are specially marked in the vocabulary (including the few that are accented on the stem vowel and not the root (cf. §14.4 and the paradigm of *tuqqā-*). Read §§21.1–21.11 on the use of active and medio-passive. Hittite has no subjunctive or optative mood. Read §§23.12–23.15 on how Hittite expresses potential or unreal conditions.

Translation Exercise

13.1. LUGAL-*uš* É.ŠÀ-*na pa-iz-zi nu-uš-ši* MUNUS.LUGAL-*aš ap-pa-an-da i-ya-at-ta*

♦ 13.2. *ma-a-an-wa A-NA* ^{URU}*Ne-ri-iq-qa pa-i-wa-ni nu-wa-aš-šan*[206] *ku-wa-pí*[207] *e-šu-wa-aš-ta*[208]

◊ 13.3. *nu-uš-ša-an ša-ra-a-az-zi-ya-aš* KUR-*e-aš kat-te-ra-aš-ša ut-ne-ya-aš ḫu-u-ma-an-da-aš tu-el-pát* ^{d}UTU-*wa-aš* <*la-lu-ki-ma-aš*> *ti-ya-ri nu* UR.GI$_7$-*aš* ŠAḪ-*aš-ša ḫa-an-ni-eš-šar ḫa-an-na-at-ta-ri*

♦ 13.4. ^{d}*A-la-lu-uš-ša-an*[206] ^{GIŠ}ŠÚ.A-*ki e-eš-zi*[208] *da-aš-šu-ša-aš-ši* ^{d}*A-nu-uš* DINGIR.MEŠ-*aš ḫa-an-te-ez-zi-ya-aš-me-iš*[209] *pé-ra-an-še-et*[210] *ar-ta*

♦ 13.5. *nu-uš-ma-aš*[211]*-kán* ^{d}10-*aš* ^{d}*Da-aš-mi-šu-uš-ša* ŠU-*za ap-pa-an-da-at*[212]

206. See §28.74 for the use of *-(š)šan*.

207. Interpret *kuwapi* here as interrogative.

208. The syntax of *ēš-* 'sit (down)' in sentences 2 and 4 is that of Old Hittite; its syntax in sentence 8 is that of NH. Read carefully §28.33.

209. See §18.15 with note 17 on the meaning of the genitive with *ḫantezzi(ya)-*.

210. See §§6.6 and §20.33 on the use of *=šet* with *pēran*.

211. *-šmaš* is functioning here as a reflexive. See §17.9.

212. See §21.8 for the reciprocal use of the medio-passive, with or without *-za*.

♦ 13.6. *ma-aḫ-ḫa-an-mu-kán*[213] LÚ.MEŠ ^{URU}*Du-uq-qa-am-ma me-na-aḫ-ḫa-*<*an*>*-da a-ú-e-er na-at-mu me-na-aḫ-ḫa-an-da ú-e-er*

♦ 13.7. [*nu-za ŠA* KUR ^{URU}]*Dur-mi-it-ta* ^{URU}*Ga-aš-ga-aš*[214] *da-a-an* EGIR*-pa*[215] ÌR*-aḫ-ta-at*[216] *nu-mu* ÉRIN.MEŠ *pé-eš-ke-u-an da-a-ir*

13.8. *ma-aḫ-ḫa-an-za*[217] *A-BU-YA* DINGIR*-LÌ-iš ki-ša-at*[218] *nu-za-kán A-NA* ^{GIŠ}GU.ZA *A-BI-YA e-eš-ḫa-at*[208]

♦ 13.9. *nu ak-kán-za ku-e-da-aš uk-tu-ri-ya-aš wa-ra-a-ni nu a-pé-e-da-aš uk-tu-ri-ya-aš a-ra-aḫ-za-an-da* 12 NINDA.GUR$_4$.RA.MEŠ GAM *ti-ya-an-zi*

◊13.10. *I-NA* UD.1.KAM*-wa-ra-aš AM-MA-TU pár-ga-u-eš-kad-da-ri I-NA* ITU.1.KAM*-ma-wa-ra-aš* IKU*-an pár-ga-u-eš-kad-da-ri*[219]

13.11. *ma-aḫ-ḫa-an-za na-aš-šu* LUGAL*-uš na-aš-ma* MUNUS.LUGAL*-aš* DINGIR*-LÌ-iš ki-ša-ri*[218] *nu šal-li a-ni-ur a-ni-ya-an-zi*

♦13.12. *ú-ga A-NA* DINGIR*-YA ku-it*[220] *i-ya-nu-un nu-mu*[221] É*-YA i-na-ni pé-ra-an pít-tu-li-ya-aš* É*-er ki-ša-at*[217]

♦13.13. *nu-kán* ^{d}*Ḫé-pa-du-uš šu-uḫ-ḫa-az kat-ta ma-uš-šu-u-wa-an-zi wa-aq-qa-ri-eš*[222] *ma-an ti-ya-at ma-na-aš-kán šu-uḫ-ḫa-az kat-ta ma-uš-ta-at*[223]

♦13.14. UDU.ŠIR*=ma*[224] *ma-a-an*[225] *ḫar-ga-eš . . . ma-a-an*[225] *da-an-ku-wa-e-es Ú-UL ku-it-ki*[226] *du-uq-qa-a-ri*

♦13.15. *ma-a-an-wa-mu* 1*-an* DUMU*-KA*[227] *pa-iš-ti ma-an-wa-ra-aš-mu* ^{LÚ}*MU-TI-YA ki-ša-ri*[217]

213. On the use of *-kan* or *-ašta* with *menaḫḫanda au(š)-*, but not with *menaḫḫanda uwa-*, see CHD L-N *menaḫḫanda* 1 a 4′ and 4 a. While "nasal reduction" is real (cf. §1.141) and should generally *not* be emended, it seems unlikely that it here applied to only one of the two instances.

214. Despite the determinative one should understand this as 'the Kaskean people' (cf. note 63 to lesson 3).

215. *āppa* here has the meaning of 'again, re-'.

216. The force of the medio-passive of transitive ÌR*-naḫḫ-* 'to subject' is "autocausative" (§21.9): 'to subject oneself' (voluntarily, at least ostensibly).

217. For *kīš-* with and without *-za* in the meaning 'become', see §§28.34–28.35.

218. This is the standard expression for referring to the death of the Hittite king or queen. The reference in the second clause of sentence 11 is to the royal funeral rites.

219. For the syntax of this sentence, see §16.24 and note 44 to §16.65. For the unexpected medio-passive, see §14.7.

220. Interpret *kuit* here as interrogative.

221. For the use of *-mu*, see §16.59.

222. For the meaning of *wakkariya-* plus infinitive, see §25.25 with note 10. The pret. 3 sg. *waqqarieš* in a NS copy for expected **waqqariet* is entirely parallel to NS pret. 3 sg. *ḫulliš* for *ḫullit* (§12.25). Cf. the reverse use of *pennit* for *penniš* (§13.25) and *(i)yannit* for *(i)yanniš* (§13.28).

223. Contrary-to-fact condition expressed by correlative *man . . . man* (see §23.15) 'If she had . . . , she would have . . .'

224. This noun (to be understood as a plural, despite the absence of an overt marker) is a topic standing outside the clause proper, which follows. One may either translate it simply as the subject of the clause or render it approximately as 'as for the rams . . .'.

225. Take *mān . . . mān* together (see vocabulary and reference).

226. *ŪL kuitki* is adverbial (see note 229 in lesson 12).

227. While it is not entirely certain how the possessive was expressed in Hittite in this NH example, it is clear that the meaning is 'one son of yours' = 'one of your sons'. On the indeterminate nature of Hittite possessive pronouns, see §17.5 after Groddek!

Vocabulary

^{d}*Alalu-* (comm.) '(the god) Alalu'
^{d}*Anu-* (comm.) '(the god) Anu'
aniur- (SÍSKUR) [228] (neut.) 'ritual'
ar-^{ttari} 'to stand, stand up'
au(š)-/ū- 'to see' (for paradigm, see §13.32)
ēš-^{ari} 'to sit (down)' (cf. §28.33)
ḫanna-^{ri} 'to litigate; to judge' (the latter sense only with the "internal/content accusative" *ḫanneššar*; cf. §16.21)
^{d}*Ḫepadu-* (comm.) '(the goddess) Hebat'
inan- (neut.) 'illness'
iya-^{ttari} 'to walk, go'
^{URU}*Gašga-* (comm.) 'Kaskean'[229]
kattera- 'lower, inferior'
kīš-^{ari} 'to happen; become' (see §§28.34–35)
lalukkima- (comm.) 'radiance, light'
man (marks unreal condition)
mān ... mān 'whether ... or' (§30.115)
mau(šš)- 'to fall' (§13.32)
pargawešš- 'to grow high, tall'
pittu̯liya- (comm.) 'worry, anxiety'
šarazzi(ya)- 'upper' (see §§4.10 and 4.36 with note 129)
^{d}*Tašmišu-* (comm.) '(the god) Tašmišu'
tuqqā-^{ri} 'be visible; to matter' (§14.4)
tunnakiš(n)- (É.ŠÀ-*(n)a-*) (neut.) 'inner chamber' (§4.89)
uktu̯ri- (pl. tantum) 'funeral pyre' (lit. 'continually (burning place)')
waqqariya- 'to fail, miss, go missing' (*not* the same as *wakkā-*^{ri} 'to lack' with non-nominative experiencer)
urā-/warā-^{ni} 'to burn' (intr.) (conjugated like *tuqqā-* ^{ri} in §14.4; for *u/warāni* instead of **u/warāri*, see §1.135)
^{GIŠ}GU.ZA 'throne'
IKU-*(n)a-* (comm.) (measure of length)
ÌR-*(n)aḫḫ-* 'to subject, make one's servant'
ITU-*(m)a-* (comm.) 'month' (= *arma-*)
^{GIŠ}ŠÚ.A-*ki(t)-* (comm.) 'chair, throne' (§4.15)
UDU.ŠIR-*a/i-* (comm.) 'ram'
UR.GI$_7$-*(n)a-* (comm.) 'dog'[230]
AMMATU 'ell, yard' (measure of length)

228. SÍSKUR can also cover Hittite *malteššar* or *mukeššar*, terms for offerings, prayers or ceremonies (see CHD sub *malteššar*).

229. The Kaška were hostile nomadic groups moving about in the north, in the area between the Hittite heartland and the Black Sea.

230. For the stem of UR.GI$_7$, see [U]R.GI$_7$-*na-a-tar* KBo 19.145 ii 23 (correct the edition by Haas and Thiel 1978: 298–9). Despite this complementation it remains uncertain whether the synchronic generic word for 'dog' is a common gender *n*-stem *kuwan-/kūn-* (cf. note 241 to §4.69).

Lesson 14

Grammar

This lesson introduces the imperative mood and numerals.

Memorize the endings of the imperative active (§11.6) and medio-passive (§11.24). Note in particular the irregular second person forms of the verbs 'go' and 'come' (§12.41). Familiarize yourself with the imperative portions of the paradigms for all other verbal stem types in chapters 12, 13 and 14.

On the use of the imperative, read §§23.5–23.8. Notice that the first person plural "voluntative" is indistinguishable from the present indicative and that the imperative second person plural is formally identical to the preterite indicative. Only context can determine the intended meaning in a given example.

Numerals are almost always written logographically in Hittite, so determining the phonetic shape of the Hittite forms is difficult. The cardinal number *šya-* 'one' and the *apparent a*-stem 'two' are inflected like the demonstrative pronouns (§§9.7 and 9.10), while *teri-* 'three' is an ordinary *i*-stem (§9.12), and *me/i(y)u-* 'four' is a *u*-stem adjective (§9.13). It is unlikely that cardinal numbers above 'four' are inflected. You need not digest all aspects of numerals, but you should note some features that are not straightforward and deserve special attention: (1) the "polyptotic" use of 1-*a*- . . . 1-*a*- for certain reciprocal uses (§9.9); (2) the syntax of cardinals with non-collectives, especially the conditions for singular vs. plural agreement (§§9.18–9.22); (3) the confusingly diverse uses of the "individuating" suffix *-ant-* to count collectives (§§9.23–9.24), merely to underscore individual members of sets (§9.27), and very likely to form **ordinals** starting with 'third' (§§9.38–9.40 and 9.42–9.43); (4) the possibility that a homophonous *-ant-* stem forms nouns for sets used appositionally (§§9.28–9.29); and (5) the unfortunate ambiguity of writings UD.numeral.KAM, etc. (§9.41).

Translation Exercise

♦ 14.1. *nu-uš-ša-an* ^{d}*Te-li-pí-nu-uš* Ì.DÙG.GA-*it pa-ap-pár-ša-an-ta* KASKAL-*ša*[231] *i-ya-an-ni*

♦ 14.2. *nu-mu* LÚ.MEŠ ^{URU}*Tap-ti-na* . . . *me-na-aḫ-ḫa-an-da ú-e-er na-at-mu* GÌR.MEŠ-*aš kat-ta-an ḫa-a-li-ya-an-da-at*

231. For the collective plural of common gender *palša-*, see §3.14.

♦14.3.[232] *nu ki-iš-ša-an me-mi-er BE-LÍ-NI-wa-an-na-aš le-e ḫar-ni-ik-ti nu-wa-an-na-aš-za* ÌR-*an-ni da-a nu-wa-an-na-aš-za* ÉRIN.MEŠ ANŠE.KUR.RA.ḪI.A *i-ya*[233]

♦ 14.4. *nu-uš-ma-aš*[234] ḪUR.SAG.MEŠ *pé-ra-an ták-ša-at-ni-ya-an-ta-ru* ÍD.ḪI.A-*ma-aš-ma-aš*[235] *pé-ra-an ar-mi-iz-zi-ya-an-ta-ru*

♦ 14.5. *nu-mu-uš-ša-an ḫu-u-ma-an-da-az pa-aḫ-ši nu ku-iš A-NA* ^{d}UTU-*ŠI i-da-a-lu-uš tu-uq-qa a-pa-a-aš i-da-a-lu-uš e-eš-du*[236]

14.6. *tu-el-kán ŠA* DINGIR-*LÌ* ŠU-*i an-da a-aš-šu lu-u-lu ú-wa-al-lu nu-mu ut-ne-e ḫu-u-ma-an-da ma-ni-ya-aḫ*

♦ 14.7. LÚ.MEŠ ^{URU}*Nu-ḫaš-ši-wa ku-it ku-u-ru-ur nu-wa-aš-ma-aš*[237] *i-it ḫal-ki*$^{\mathrm{HI.A}}$*uš*[238] *ar-ḫa ḫar-ni-ik nu-wa-ra-aš-kán an-da ḫa-at-ke-eš-nu-ut*

♦ 14.8. *nu mi-e-ú-uš*[239] *ku-i-uš* ^{d}UTU-*uš tu-u-ri-ya-an ḫar-ši nu-uš-ma-aš ka-a-ša*[240] DUMU.NAM.LÚ.U$_{19}$.LU-*aš ḫal-ki-in šu-uḫ-ḫa-aš nu mi-e-wa-aš-ti-iš*[241] *ka-ri-ip-pa-an-du nu ku-it-ma-an mi-e-ya-wa-aš-te-eš*[241] *ḫal-ki-in ka-ri-ip-pa-an-zi zi-ga* ^{d}UTU-*uš ḫu-e-eš*

14.9. *A-NA* ^{d}UTU-*ŠI-za*[242] *ag-ga-an-na-aš* TI-*an-na-aš* UN-*aš e-eš*

♦ 14.10. *ki-nu-na-wa ka-a-ša*[240] DINGIR-*LU*$_{4}$[243] 2 TA.ÀM *šar-ni-ik-ta nu BE-EL* SÍSKUR *pár-ku-iš nam-ma e-eš-du*

♦ 14.11. *ták-ku* DUMU LUGAL *ḫa-an-te-ez-zi-iš* NU.GÁL *nu ku-iš ta-a-an pé-e-da-aš* DUMU-*RU nu* LUGAL-*uš a-pa-a-aš ki-ša-ru*

♦ 14.12. *nu ma-a-an ku-u-uš li-in-ga-a-uš pa-aḫ-ḫa-aš-du-ma šu-ma-a-ša* DINGIR.MEŠ-*eš pa-aḫ-ša-an-da-ru*

◊ 14.13. *nu-wa-mu-za* DUMU-*la-an ku-it ḫal-ze-eš-še-eš-ta*[244] *ki-nu-na-wa e-ḫu nu-wa za-aḫ-ḫi-ya-wa-aš-ta-ti*[245] *nu-wa-an-na-aš* ^{d}10 *BE-LÍ-YA* DI-*eš-šar ḫa-an-na-a-ú*

14.14. *ma-a-an-kán ku-u-un li-in-ga-in šar-ra-at-ta nu-ut-ta li-in-ki-ya-aš* DINGIR.MEŠ *QA-DU* DAM-*KA* DUMU.MEŠ-*KA da-an-ku-ya-az ták-na-az ar-ḫa ḫar-ni-in-kán-du*[246]

232. This sentence immediately follows sentence 2 in the original context.

233. This shows the use of *iya-* with a double accusative in the sense 'to make X (into) Y' (§§16.16 and 16.18). The same syntax is found in sentence 13 below.

234. Interpret *-šmaš* in both occurrences in this example as *second* person plural dative.

235. The use of *=ma* here is to mark the second of contrastive topics (cf. §29.35). It is not the contrastive focus particle and clearly not adversative 'but'.

236. The Hittites often define 'good' and 'evil' in a highly subjective fashion. Here *idālu-* is effectively 'inimical' or *persona non grata*.

237. For the use of the dative enclitic pronoun to indicate possession, see §16.59.

238. For the unusual spelling, see §32.13.

239. The Sungod was believed to have a team of four horses. The spelling *mi-e-* is probably to be read as /me:-/.

240. For the meaning of *kāša*, see §§17.47–17.50.

241. The forms *mi-e-wa-aš* and *mi-e-ya-wa-aš* must be taken in context as nominative plural common gender. Their status as real forms of a *u*-stem is extremely dubious. The text copy from which this passage is taken shows a number of unexpected spellings and inflections (notice the unique and aberrant *-pp-* of the forms of *karap-*). Read *-ti-iš* in the first example as if it were *-te-eš* like the second.

242. On the reason for *-za* here, see §28.41.

243. DINGIR-*LU*$_{4}$ stands here for an accusative. On this phenomenon, see note 11 to §1.5.

244. For the use of *-za* plus *ḫalzišša-*, see §28.29.

245. For this use of the medio-passive, see §21.8.

246. This rather frequent collocation of ablative and 'destroy' in curse formulas is elliptical. English 'to wipe from' captures the sense.

♦ 14.15. NIM.LÀL[247] *te-ri-ya-aš* UD-*aš*[248] *mi-u-wa-aš* UD-*aš*[248] KASKAL-*an pa-a-an-du*

♦ 14.16. *nu I-NA* ^{URU}*A-ri-ip-ša-a an-da-*[*an za-aḫ-ḫi-ya i-ya-an*]*-ni-*[*ya-nu-un*][249] *a-ši-ma-kán* ^{URU}*A-ri-ip-ša-aš* [ŠÀ A.A]B.BA *ki-it-ta-ri*

♦ 14.17. *nu-uš-ša-*[*an ḫa-a*]*n-te-ez-zi-ya* ^{GIŠ}BANŠUR-*i ku-iš* 1 NINDA.GUR$_4$.RA *ki-it-ta-at* . . . *na-an-ša-an A-NA* ^{GIŠ}BANŠUR.GAL . . . *še-er da-a-i*

Vocabulary

andan 'into, unto' (postposition; NH only)
armizziya- 'to bridge'
aši 'that, yonder' (distal demonstrative; (see §§7.9–7.14 and 17.40)
eḫu 'come!' (imp. 2 sg. to *uwa-*; §12.41)
ḫaliya-^{ri} 'to bow, prostrate oneself'
ḫatkešnu- 'besiege, hem in' (+ *anda*)
ḫue/iš- 'to live, be alive'
īt/ītten 'go!' (imp. 2 sg./pl. to *pāi-*; §12.41)
ki-^{ttari} 'to lie, be placed' (cf. §21.17)
lūlu- (neut.) 'prosperity'
me(i)u- 'four'
papparš- 'to sprinkle'
parā ḫand(ant)ātar (neut.) 'divine favor, providence'
šarra-^{ttari} 'to transgress'
šuḫḫa-^{ḫḫi} 'to pour (out)' (invariant *a*-stem; §13.12)
takšatniya-/takšanniya- 'to (make) level' (see §1.126)
teri- 'three'
^{GIŠ}BANŠUR.GAL 'large table'
Ì.DÙG.GA 'fine oil'
ÌR-*(n)ātar* (neut.) 'servitude, bondage, slavery'
NIM.LÀL-*a-* (comm.) 'bee'
ŠÀ = Akkad. *INA* 'in, on, at'
TA.ÀM 'time(s)' (with numbers)

247. NIM.LÀL stands for a plural, although it is not marked as such.

248. The apparent singular agreement with a common gender noun with inanimate referent with 'three' and 'four' violates the rule established by Rizza and Rieken (cf. §9.18), but in a NS copy of an OH text this may be a purely orthographic problem. That is, UD-*aš* and the agreeing numerals may well be genitive *plural*: cf. *nu* ^{URU}*Nēši* URU.DIDLI *wetenun* URU-*yan ā*[*p*(*pa*)*n*] . . . 'I built fortifications in Nesas; be[hind] the fortifications (gen. pl.!) . . . KBo 3.22 55 (Anitta; OH/OS).

249. In NH the originally strictly inceptive *(i)yanna/i-* 'to set out, start walking' comes to take a goal and mean 'to march to/toward' (here 'against').

COMPREHENSIVE VOCABULARY

This list includes all vocabulary introduced in the lessons. It makes no claim to cover meanings of the listed words appropriate to texts outside this tutorial. The alphabetization follows the usual conventions for Hittite, with Hittite, Sumerian and Akkadian in separate sections. In the Hittite section the voiced stops *b*, *d* and *g* are alphabetized with *p*, *t* and *k* respectively. Geminate consonants are treated like single consonants. Since we transliterate the glides with *w* and *y*, we have alphabetized according to the usual place of these letters. In the transliteration of Sumerograms we have generally followed the practice of the *HZL*. We have also included alternate or superseded readings for some common Sumerograms, since readers will meet with them in Hittitological works (for more complete coverage of these, see Tischler 2001). The citing of phonetic complements in the forms given below does not mean that such complements are always present. In the case of complements part of which is enclosed in parentheses (e.g., UN-*(š)a-*), the full form is often not employed. Numbers in parentheses following the glosses refer to the lesson in which the word with that meaning first appears in the exercises.

Hittite (Including Luwianisms)

-a (conj.) (geminates preceding consonant)/*-ya* (after vowel) 'and; also' (see Latin *-que*) (1)

-a (conj.) (non-geminating)/*-ma* (introduces new topic; see Greek *δέ*); 'but, on the other hand, while' (weakly adversative, often contrastive/oppositional; see CHD *-ma*); (1)

aiš- (KA×U-*iš*) (neut.) 'mouth' (8)

āk-/akk-^{ḫḫi} 'to die' (8)

^{d}*Alalu-* (comm.) '(the god) Alalu' (13)

alpa- (comm.) 'cloud' (2)

anna- (AMA-*(n)a-*) (comm.) 'mother' (1)

aniur-(SÍSKUR)[250] (neut.) 'ritual' (13)

aniya- 'to carry out, execute; write' (10)

250. SÍSKUR can also cover Hittite *malteššar* or *mukeššar*, terms for offerings, prayers or ceremonies (see CHD sub *malteššar*).

anda 'in(to); in, among' (4, 7)
andan 'into, unto' (14)
antuḫša- (UN-*(š)a-*/LÚ.U$_{19}$.LU-*a-*) (comm.) 'man, human being' (1)
^{d}*Anu-* (comm.) '(the god) Anu' (13)
āppa (EGIR-*pa*) 'back; again' (3)
āppan (EGIR-*an*) 'behind, after' (*āppan tiya-* 'to step behind' = 'to support') (9)
appanda (EGIR-*(p)anda*) 'behind; afterwards' (6)
apeniššan (*QATAMMA*) 'thus, so' (2)
appezzi(ya)- (EGIR-*(ez)zi(ya)-*) 'rear; last' (2)
appezzian 'afterwards' (old nom.-acc. sg.neuter of *appezziya-* used adverbially) (12)
appezziyaz (EGIR-*(ezziy)az*) 'afterwards; later' (2)
ā/ar-^{ḫḫi} 'to arrive (in), reach' (+ d.-l. or allative) (8)
ar-^{ttari} 'to stand, stand up' (13)
araḫzanda 'around' (6)
arḫa 'away, off' (preverb) (1)
ariya- 'to make (the subject of) an oracular inquiry' (10)
arkam(m)an- (comm.) 'tribute' (7)
arkam(m)anātar (neut.) 'payment of tribute' (7)
armizziya- 'to bridge' (14)
aruna- (A.AB.BA) (comm.) 'sea' (4)
aš(ša)nu- 'to make right; arrange' (4)
ašāwar (TÙR) (neut.) 'sheepfold' (7)
ašeššar (neut.) 'assembly' (7)
aši 'that' (pron.) (see §§7.9–7.14 and 17.40–43) (14)
āššiyant- 'dear, beloved' (5)
āššu- 'good'; as neuter collective noun 'goods' (see §3.24, end, for the spelling *āššū* and its idiomatic sense) (3)
atta- (*ABU/ABI*) (comm.) 'father'(1)
au(š)-/ū- 'to see' (for paradigm, see §13.32) (13)
awan katta 'down beside' (9)
eḫu 'come!' (imp. 2 sg. to *uwa-*) (14)
eku-/aku- 'to drink' (paradigm in §12.3) (1)
ēpp-/app- 'to take, seize, grasp; hold' (paradigm in §12.3) (1)
e/išḫarwant- 'bloody; blood-red' (11)
ēš-/aš- A 'to be' (paradigm in §12.3) (1)
ēš-/aš- B 'to be sitting, reside' (see §28.33) (1)
ēš-^{ari} 'to sit (down)' (13)
ēšša- (see *īšša-*)
ēšḫar (neut.) 'blood; bloodshed' (6)
ēd-/ad- 'to eat' (paradigm in §12.3) (1)
ḫāli- (neut.) 'corral' (7)
^{LÚ}*ḫalliri-* (comm.) (cult functionary) (4)
ḫališšiya- 'to coat, inlay' (7)
ḫaliya-^{ri} 'to bow, prostrate oneself' (also active in NH) (2, 14)
ḫalki- (comm.) 'grain; barley' (2)
ḫallu- 'deep' (3)

^{LÚ}*ḫalugattalla-* (comm.) 'messenger' (7)
ḫalzai-$^{\underline{ḫḫi}}$ 'to call, summon' (12)
ḫalziššа-$^{\underline{ḫḫi}}$ (pluractional stem to *ḫalzai-* 'to call'; see §13.14) (11)
ḫamešḫa- (Ú.BURU$_7$, *DĪŠĪ*) (comm.) 'spring' (11)
ḫanna- (comm.) 'grandmother' (8)
ḫanna-^{ri} and *ḫanna-*$^{\underline{ḫḫi}}$ 'to judge' (13 and 14)
^{d}*Ḫannaḫanna-* (^{d}NIN.TU) (a fate-goddess) (10)
ḫanneššar (DI, *DĪNU*) (neut.) 'judgment, law case' (8, 13)
ḫandāi- 'to arrange, prepare' (3)
^{d}*Ḫantašepa-* (comm.) (one of class of minor deities) (9)
ḫantezzi(ya)- (IGI-*(ez)zi(ya)-*) 'front, foremost; first' (2)
ḫapan- (ÍD-*an-*) (comm.) 'river' (8)
ḫappiriya- (URU-*(riy)a-*) (comm.) 'city' (2)
ḫāran-^{MUŠEN} (TI$_8$/Á^{MUŠEN}) (comm.) 'eagle' (7)
ḫarātar 'offense' (12)
ḫāriya- (comm.) 'valley' (3)
ḫariya- 'to bury' (7)
ḫar(k)- 'to hold, have' (paradigm in §12.10) (6)
ḫark- 'to perish' (2) (+ *arḫa* 'perish utterly, be destroyed') (12)
ḫarki- (BABBAR) 'white' (2)
ḫarnāu- (comm.) 'birthing stool' (§4.48) (6)
ḫarnink- 'to destroy' (with or without *arḫa*) (5)
ḫaršar (SAG.DU) (neut.) 'head; person' (6)
^{NINDA}*ḫarši-* (NINDA.GUR$_4$.RA-*i-*) (comm.) 'leavened bread' (3)
^{DUG}*ḫaršiyalli-* (neut.) 'pithos, storage jar' (10)
ḫāš-/ḫašš- and *ḫeš(š)-*$^{\underline{ḫḫi}}$ 'to open (tr.)' (with or without *āppa*) (8)
ḫāš-/ḫašš-$^{\underline{ḫḫi}}$ 'to give birth' (optional *-za*) (8)
ḫašša- (GUNNI-*a-*) (comm.) 'hearth' (3)
ḫa(š)šātar (MÁŠ-*tar*) (neut.) 'birth; family' (6)
ḫaštāi- (neut.) 'bone' (9)
ḫaššu- (LUGAL-*u-*) (comm.) 'king' (3)
ḫaššuššara- (MUNUS.LUGAL-*(r)a-*) (comm.) 'queen' (1).
ḫatalkiš(n)- (neut.) 'hawthorn' (11)
ḫattātar (neut.) 'wisdom; wise thought, wise plan, strategy' (9)
ḫatkešnu- 'besiege, hem in' (+ *anda*) (14)
ḫatrāi- 'to send a message (about), write (about)' (3)
ḫenkan- (neut.) 'death; plague' (7)
^{d}*Ḫepadu-* (comm.) 'Hebat' (13)
ḫimma- (comm.) 'model, replica' (7)
EZEN$_4$ *ḫišuwa-* (a major festival) (10)
ḫuḫḫa- (comm.) 'grandfather; forefather' (8)
ḫue/iš- (TI-*eš-*) 'to live, be alive' (14)
ḫuišnu- (TI-*nu-*) 'to keep alive; rescue, save' (2)
ḫuišwant- (TI-*(w)ant-*) 'alive, living' (6)
ḫuišwātar (TI-*(wa)tar*) (neut.) 'life' (6)
ḫuett(iya)- 'to draw, pull' (11)

ḫuitar (neut.) ‘game, wildlife’, (pl. *ḫuidār* ‘wild animals, beasts’), see §4.110 (6)
ḫulli/u/a- ‘to fight (someone, -thing); contravene’ (§12.26) (6)
ḫūmant- ‘all, whole’ (usually follows modified noun but, see §§18.8–18.9) (5)
ḫūnink- ‘to injure’(5)
ḫūppar- (comm.) ‘bowl’ (8)
ḫurki- (comm.) ‘wheel’ (2)
ḫūdāk ‘immediately; suddenly’ (2)
ḫuwai-^{ḫḫi} ‘to stir, move (intr.); flee’ (9)
ḫuwappa- (ḪUL-*(p)a-*) ‘wicked, evil’ (2)
inan- (neut.) ‘illness’ (13)
irḫa- (ZAG-*a-*) (comm.) ‘border (territory)’ (4)
īšša-/ēšša-^{ḫḫi} (pluractional stem to *iya-* ‘to do, make’) (paradigm in §13.14) (11)
išḫā- (EN-*a-*, *BELU*) (comm.) ‘lord, master; owner’ (2)
išḫaḫru- (neut.) ‘tears’ (6)
išḫai-^{ḫḫi} ‘to bind, tie; impose’ (12)
išḫiul- (*RIKILTU*) (neut.) ‘obligation, treaty’ (8)
išpai-^{ḫḫi} (with *-za*) ‘to be satisfied’ (9)
išpant- (GE$_6$-*ant-*, *MŪŠU*) (comm.) ‘night’ (5)
išpā/ant-^{ḫḫi} (see *ši(p)pā/ant-* ^{ḫḫi})
^{DUG}*išpantuzzi-* (neut.) ‘libation-vessel’ (9)
ištamašš- (GEŠTU) ‘to hear’ (5)
ištanana- (ZAG.GAR.RA-*(n)a-*) ‘altar, sacrificial table’ (2)
^{d}*Ištanu-* (^{d}UTU-*u-*) (comm.) ‘the sun-(god)’ (4)
ištanzan- (ZI-*an-*) (comm.) ‘soul’ (8)
ištarna arḫa ‘through, across’ (postposition with accusative) (4)
ištarnink- ‘to make sick, incapacitate’ (5)
īt/ītten ‘go!’ (imp. 2 sg./pl. to *pai-*) (14)
idālawaḫḫ- ‘to mistreat, harm’ (12)
idālawešš- ‘to become bad/hostile’ (4)
idālu- (ḪUL-*(l)u-*) ‘bad, evil; hostile’ (3)
iwar ‘as, like’ (with preceding genitive) (4)
iya- ‘to do, make; treat (as)’; + *-za* ‘to worship’ (2)
iya-^{ttari} (GIN-^{ttari}) ‘to walk, go’ (13)
iyanna/i-^{ḫḫi} ‘to set out; begin to move; go’ (11)
kaka- (ZU$_{19}$) (comm.) ‘tooth’ (12)
kallar(a)- ‘unfavorable, harmful’ (6)
ganešš- ‘to recognize, acknowledge’ (3)
kā/ank-^{ḫḫi} ‘to hang’ (tr.) (8)
karā/ep-^{ḫḫi} ‘to devour’ (9)
kāri tiya- ‘to accede to (the wishes of)’ (7)
karp-/karpiya- ‘to lift, raise; perform, carry out’ (1) and (8)
karš- ‘to cut; segregate’ (7)
karšanu- ‘to omit, neglect’ (2)
kartimmiešš- ‘to become angry’ (3)
kartimmiyatt- (TUKU.TUKU-*(at)t-*) (comm.) ‘anger’ (5)
kartimmiyawant- (TUKU.TUKU-*(w)ant-*) ‘angry’ (5)

karū 'formerly, earlier; already' (12)
karuwili- 'former; primeval' (2)
kāša/kāšma (4) (see §§17.47–17.50)
^{URU}*Gašga-* (comm.) 'Kaskean' (13)
katta^{1} (this and the following entry usually spelled *kat-ta*, sometimes *ka-at-ta*, Sum. GAM) 'down(ward)' (3)
katta^{2} 'with, beside' (9)
kattan^{1} (this and the the following entry usually spelled *kat-ta-an*, sometimes *ka-at-ta-an*, Sum. GAM-*an*) 'below, under' (7)
kattan^{2} 'with, beside' (12)
kattanda 'down in(to)' (9)
kattera- 'lower' (13)
gēnu- (neut.) 'knee' (3)
genzuwala- 'merciful' (4)
**kēr* (ŠÀ) (neut.) 'heart' (§4.120) (9)
ke/iššara- and *keššar-* (ŠU-*(r)a-*, *QATU*) (comm.) 'hand' (1) and (8) (for stem and inflection, see §4.80)
ki-^{ttari} 'to lie, be placed' (14)
kinun 'now' (12)
kīš-^{ari} (DÙ-^{ari}) 'to happen; become' (13)
kiššan 'thus, as follows' (3)
kištant- (comm.) 'hunger' (10)
kištanu- 'to extinguish' (6)
kuen-/kun- 'to strike' (without *-kkan*); 'to kill' (with *-kkan*) (1)
kuer-/kur- 'to cut' (1)
$^{A.ŠÀ}$*kuera-* (comm.) 'field' (2)
kuit 'because, since' (3)
kuitman 'while, as long as; until' (9)
gulšš- 'to incise, inscribe, draw' (6)
kunna- (ZAG-*(n)a-*) 'right-(hand)' (adj.) (1)
^{TÚG}*kureššar* (neut.) 'scarf' (8)
kūrur- 'hostility; hostile' (see §§4.85–86) (8)
kuššanka 'ever', *natta kuššanka* = 'never' (7)
kuwapi 'where; when (NH only)' (interrog. or rel.) (10)
kuwapikki 'anywhere; any time' (12)
kuwat 'why?' (2)
kuwatta šer 'on what account, why' (10)
lāḫḫa- (comm.) 'campaign; trip' (12)
laḫ(ḫ)anzan-^{MUŠEN} (comm.) (kind of duck) (7)
lāi- (DU$_{8}$) 'to release, let go' (12)
lāk-^{ḫḫi} 'to knock down/out' (12)
lalukkima- (ZALAG.GA-*a-*) (comm.) 'radiance, light' (13)
lāman (*ŠUM*) (neut.) 'name' (7)
lē (plus indicative) 'do/shall not' (prohibitive negative) (2)
lēlaniya-^{ttari} 'to become angry' (8)
lēliwant- 'swift' (7)

le/išš- 'to gather, pick up' (9)
lingāi- (*NĪŠ* DINGIR-*LÌ*) (comm.) 'oath' (10)
linkiyanteš (*NĪŠ* DINGIR.MEŠ) (comm. pl.) 'the oaths' (7)
lukke/a- 'to set fire to' (§12.21) (6)
lūlu- (neut.) 'prosperity' (14)
luluwāi- 'to make prosper' (4)
luttāi- ([GIŠ]AB) (neut.) 'window(s)' (9)
luzzi- (neut.) 'compulsory public work, corvée' (8)
māḫḫan (GIM-*an*) 'as, like' (2); 'when; as' (4); 'how?'
makkešš- 'to multiply, become numerous' (intrans.) (3)
man (marks unreal condition) (13)
mān 'if, whenever' (in Old Hittite also 'when') (1)
mān . . . *mān* 'whether . . . or' (see §30.114) (13)
maniyaḫḫ- 'to hand over; administer' (12)
māša- ($BURU_5$) (comm.) 'locust' (9)
mau(šš)- 'to fall' (13)
mēḫur (neut.) 'time' (6)
me(i)u- 'four' (14)
mekki- 'much, many'; nom.-acc. sg. neuter as adverb 'very' (2) and (5)
mema/i-[ḫḫi] (DU_{11}) 'to speak', pluractional stem *memiške-* (7, 12)
memi(y)an- (INIM) (comm.) 'word; matter, affair' (7)
menaḫḫanda (IGI-*anda*) 'towards, facing' (postposition with dat.-loc.) (4)
[LÚ]*mene(y)a-* (comm.) (a cult functionary) (11)
[d]*Mezzulla-* (comm.) (a deity) (5)
[(URU)]*Mizra/i* 'Egypt' (3)
naḫ(ḫ)-[ḫḫi] 'to be afraid' (12)
naḫšaratt- (comm.) 'fear, awe; fearsomeness' (5)
naḫšariya- 'to be(come) afraid' (4)
naḫšarnu- 'to frighten, terrify, scare' (1)
nai-[ḫḫi] 'to turn; send' (§13.23) (9)
nakkī- 'heavy; important; revered, august' (2)
namma (clause-initial) 'then, next'; (non-initial) 'again' (*ŪL namma* 'no longer') (2, 3)
nanna/i-[ḫḫi] 'to drive' (11)
našma 'or' (4)
naššu . . . *našma* 'either . . . or' (9)
nāta- (GI) (comm.) 'reed; arrow' (11)
natta 'not' (usually written as *ŪL* or *UL*, rarely NU) (1)
nekut- (comm.) 'twilight, evening' (6)
nēpiš- (AN, *ŠAMÊ*) (neut.) 'heaven, sky' (8)
nēwa- (GIBIL) 'new' (3)
nink- 'to raise, mobilize; (re)move' (5)
nu (conj.) (marks beginning of a clause; indicates progression of the action; sometimes 'and (then)', but often best left untranslated in English) (1)
nūman (marks negative volition of subject; translatable as 'do/did not wish to . . .'; §26.17) (10)

nuntarnu- 'to hasten, act hastily' (4)
paḫ(ḫa)š- 'to protect' (6)
paḫḫašnu-, *paḫšanu-* (PAP-*nu-*) 'to protect, guard' (with d.-l. and *peran* 'against . . .') (1)
paḫḫur (IZI) (neut.) 'fire' (6)
pai- 'to go' (4)
pai-^{ḫḫi} 'to give' (9)
palša- (KASKAL-*(š)a-*) (comm.) 'path, way; time, instance' (11)
paltana- (^{UZU}ZAG.LU-*(n)a-*) (comm.) 'shoulder' (2)
papparš- 'to sprinkle' (14)
paprātar (neut.) 'impurity' (6)
parā 'forth, out' (preverb) (1)
parā ḫand(ant)ātar (neut.) 'divine favor, providence' (14)
parḫ- 'to chase; attack' (2) and (11)
parā-^{ḫḫi} 'to appear, come forth' (9)
pargawešš- 'to grow high, tall' (13)
parku- 'high' (3)
parkui- 'pure' (3)
parkunu- 'to purify, cleanse' (6)
-pat (particle) (see §28.119 and following) (6)
pada- (GÌR-*a-*) (comm.) 'foot' (1)
$^{GI/GIŠ}$*pattar* (neut.) 'basket' (9)
pē ḫar(k)- 'to offer, furnish' (7)
peḫute/u/a- 'to lead' (§12.23) (7)
penna/i-^{ḫḫi} 'to drive (away)' (§13.18) (11)
**pēr/parn-* (É) (neut.) 'house' (§4.119) (6)
pēran 'before, in front of' (1)
pēda- (neut.) 'place, spot' (2)
pēda-^{ḫḫi} 'to carry (off), bring' (10)
pišena/i- (LÚ-*(n)a/i-*) (comm.) 'man, male person' (but cf. §4.73) (1)
pittu̱liya- (comm.) 'worry, anxiety' (13)
pittuliyant- 'worried, anxious' (5)
piya- 'to send' (5)
GUD *pūḫugari-* (comm.) 'ox of ritual substitution' (10)
punušš- (ÈN.TAR) 'to ask, question, interrogate' (2)
šai-^{ḫḫi} 'to press; seal' (9) (but see §13.30!)
šā/ekk-^{ḫḫi} (Akk. *IDI*) 'to know; recognize' (8)
šakl(ā)i- (comm.) 'custom, rule; prerogative, right; rite, ceremony (as the prerogative of a deity)' (9)
šāktāi- 'to tend to, care for' (the sick or injured) (5)
šākuwi- (IGI-*i-*) (comm.) 'eye' (6) (but with coll. pl. *šākuwa*!)
šallešš- (GAL-*(l)ešš-*) 'to grow large; to grow up' (3)
šalli- (GAL-*(l)i-*) 'great, large; adult' (2)
šanezzi- 'fine; sweet' (5)
šanḫ- (a) (with no particle) 'to seek, look for; attempt, try;' (b) (w. *-kan* or *-ašta*) 'to search through, scour, sweep' (5)

^{LÚ}*šankunni-* (^{LÚ} SANGA-*(n)i-*) (comm.) 'priest' (3)
šarā 'up(ward)' (4)
šarra-^{ttari} (with *-kan* or *-ašta*) 'to traverse, transgress' (14)
šarazzi(ya)- (UGU-*(az)zi(ya)-*) 'upper' (13)
šarku- 'exalted, eminent, powerful' (4)
šarlāi- 'to exalt, praise, vindicate' (3)
šarnikzil- (comm. and neut.) 'restitution' (8)
šarnink- 'to make restitution (acc. = for something)' (6)
šardi(y)a- (*NĀRĀRU*) (comm.) 'helper, auxiliary' (8)
šāru- (neut.) 'booty, plunder' (3)
šaruwāi- 'to plunder' (3)
šašt- (^{GIŠ}NÁ) (comm.) 'bed; sleep' (5)
šēli- (comm.) 'grain heap, granary' (10)
šer 'above; on; for' (with preceding dative-locative) (5)
ši(p)pā/and-/išpā/and-^{ḫḫi} (BAL) 'to libate; with *-kan* 'to sacrifice, offer to' (8)
šiun(i)- (DINGIR-*LÌ-n(i)-*) (comm.) 'god' (2)
šīwatt- (UD/UD.KAM-*(at)t-*) 'day' (5)
šiyeššar (KAŠ-*eššar*) 'beer' (6)
šuḫḫa- (comm.) 'roof' (4)
šuḫḫa-^{ḫḫi} 'to pour (out)' (14)
šumeš 'you' (pl.) (1)
šunna-^{ḫḫi} 'to fill' (10)
šūniya- 'to sow, scatter, sprinkle' (5)
^{UZU}*šuppa-* 'sacralized/consecrated meat' (collective plural only) (4)
šuppi- 'holy, sacred, consecrated' (2)
šūwe/a- 'to push (away), reject' (§12.21) (6)
ta (conj.) (Old Hittite only; see §§29.10–29.13) (5)
dā-^{ḫḫi} 'to take' (+ *parā* 'to pick out') (10)
dai-^{ḫḫi} 'to put, place' (9)
tak(ki)š- 'to put together, make, perpetrate; wield' (§12.14) (12)
takšan 'together' (1)
takšatniya-/takšanniya- 'to (make) level' (14)
takšul- (neut.) 'peace' (8)
takšulatar (neut.) 'peace' (7)
takku 'if' (Old Hittite only) (5)
daluki- 'long' (5)
tamašš- 'to press, oppress' (7)
dān 'a second time' (12)
dannatta- 'empty, desolate' (12)
taninu- 'to put in order, organize' (9)
dankui- (GE_6-*i-*) 'dark, black' (2)
dandukiš(n)- (neut.) 'mortality' = NAM.LÚ.U_{19}.LU; *dandukišnaš* DUMU-*(l)a-* 'child of mortality' = 'human being' (also written DUMU.NAM.LÚ.U_{19}.LU-*(l)a-*) (11)
tar- (see *tē-*)
tarḫu-/taruḫ- (with *-za*) 'to overcome'; (without *-za*) 'be superior' (§12.12) (3)

tarku-/taruk- 'to dance' (§12.12) (4)
tarmāi- 'to nail, fasten' (3)
tarna/i-^{ḫḫi} 'to release, let go' (11)
tarpašša- (comm.) 'ritual substitute' (5)
tāru- (GIŠ-*(r)u-*) (neut.) 'wood; tree' (3)
daš(ša)nu- 'to make powerful' (3)
^{d}*Tašmišu-* (comm.) '(the god) Tasmisu' (13)
daššešš- 'to become powerful' (3)
daššu- 'mighty, powerful' (3)
dašuwaḫḫ- 'to blind' (12)
tāye/a- 'to steal' (§12.21) (2)
tē-/tar- 'to speak; mention' (6) (§12.46)
tēkan (KI) (neut.) 'earth' (§4.68) (7)
^{d}*Telipinu-* (comm.) (a male deity of the storm-god class, generally conceived as the producer of life and proliferation among plants and animals) (7)
tēpawešš- 'to become (too) small' (5)
teri- 'three' (14)
tešḫa- (Ù) (comm.) 'dream' (5)
te/iššummi- (GAL) (comm.) 'cup' (7)
tit(ta)nu- 'to install' (+ *arḫa* 'to remove [from a position]') (11)
tiya- 'to step; station oneself' (2)
tuegga- (NÍ.TE) (comm.) 'body; limb' (3)
^{LÚ}*tūḫukantaḫit-* 'position of crown-prince' (see §§2.17 and 4.15) (11)
tuqqā-^{ri} 'to be visible; to matter' (§14.4) (13)
tunnakiš(n)- (É.ŠÀ-*(n)a-*) (neut.) 'inner chamber' (13)
tuppi- (Sum. DUB, Akkad. *ṬUPPU*) (neut.) 'clay tablet' (3)
tūriya- 'to hitch/yoke up' (11)
dušgaratt- (comm.) 'joy' (5)
duddumili 'secretly' (6)
d/tuwarni- 'to break' (in OH a *mi*-verb, in NH mostly replaced by *ḫi*-inflection; see paradigm in §12.26) (11)
tuzziya- 'to encamp, go into camp' (5)
uktūri- (pl. tantum) 'funeral pyre' (13)
unu- 'to adorn' (also inflected as a stem *unuwāi-*) (5)
uppa/i-^{ḫḫi} 'to send' (11)
uppeššar (neut.) 'thing sent, gift' (12)
uda-^{ḫḫi} 'to bring' (10)
uttar (Sum. INIM, Akkad. *AWAT*, pl. *AWATE*) (neut.) 'word; matter, affair' (6)
utnē- (KUR) (neut.) 'land, country' (§4.52) (9)
uwa-, *ue-* 'to come' (4)
uwate- 'to bring' (a person) (§12.23) (9)
-wa (*-war-* before vowel) (quotative particle) (introduces direct speech) (see §§28.2–28.18) (2)
waḫnu- (BAL-*nu-*) 'to turn (usually tr.); change, alter' (10)
wāi- (neut.) 'woe' (10)
wāk-^{ḫḫi} 'to bite' (11)

waqqariya- 'to fail, miss, go missing' (see note 248 in lesson 13) (13)
wal(a)ḫ- (GUL-*aḫḫ-*) 'to strike, hit' (1)
walwa/i- (UR.MAḪ-*a/i-*) (comm.) 'lion'(1)
u/warā-^{ni} 'to burn' (intr.) (13)
warḫunu- 'to make rough, bushy' (1)
warnu- (BIL-*nu-*) 'to burn' (tr.); + *arḫa* 'to burn up' (2)
warp- 'to bathe' (10)
wāš-^{ḫḫi} 'to buy' (8)
waššе/a- 'to put on' (clothing) (+ *-za* = on oneself) (§12.21) (11)
wašta-^{ḫḫi} 'to sin' (10)
waštul- (neut.) 'sin' (8)
wātar (Sum. A, Akkad. *MÊ*) (neut.) 'water' (6)
watku- 'to spring, jump' (+ *peran arḫa* 'to flee from') (9)
wellu- (Ú.SAL-*u-*) (comm.) 'meadow, pasture' (3)
wemiya- 'to find'; + *anda* 'to reach, attain, overtake' (2)
weriya- 'to call, summon' (2)
wēštara- (^{LÚ}SIPA-*a-*) (comm.) 'shepherd'(10)
wētt-/wītt- (MU/MU.KAM-*t-*) (comm.) 'year' (§4.95) (5)
wete-/weda-^{ḫḫi} 'to build' (see §12.23 with note 118) (12)
wil(a)n- (IM) (comm.) 'clay' (7)
wi/eda(i)- 'to bring' (see note 118 to §12.23) (11)
wiyana- (GEŠTIN-*(n)a-*) (comm.) 'wine' (1)
-za ('reflexive' particle) (see §§28.19–28.48) (1)
zāḫ-/zaḫḫ—^{ḫḫi} 'to strike' (+ *anda* 'to penetrate') (8)
zaḫḫāi- (comm.) 'battle' (9)
zaḫḫiya- 'to fight' (5)
zanu- 'to cook' (trans.) (1)
zašḫāi- (Ù) (comm.) 'dream' (12)
zašḫiya- (Ù) 'to appear in a dream' (12)
zikke- 'to place' (pluractional stem to *dai-*^{ḫḫi}) (7)
^{LÚ} *zinḫuri-* (comm.) (a cult functionary) (4)

Sumerograms

A.AB.BA = *aruna-* (comm.) 'sea' (4)
A.ŠÀ-*(n)a-* (comm.) 'field' (1)
ALAM (neut.) 'image, figurine' (probably *ēš(ša)ri-* but more than one word behind the Sumerogram is possible) (8)
AMA-*a-* = *anna-* 'mother' (1)
AN = *nepiš-*, Akkad. *ŠAMÊ* 'heaven, sky' (8)
AN.ZA.GÀR 'tower' (12)
ANŠE-*a/i-* (comm.) 'ass, donkey' (11) (previously read as ANŠU)
ANŠE.GÌR.NUN.NA-*a-* (comm.) 'mule' (11) (previously read as ANŠU.GÌR.NUN.NA)
ANŠE.KUR.RA-*u-* (comm.) 'horse' (3) (previously read as ANŠU.KUR.RA)

^{LÚ}AZU 'exorcist' (3)
BA.ÚŠ 'died' (= *akkiš*) (4) (previously read as BA.BAD or BA.UG$_6$)
BABBAR = *ḫarki-* 'white' (2) (previously read as UD)
^{GIŠ}BANŠUR-*u-* (comm.) 'table' (8), ^{GIŠ}BANŠUR.GAL 'large table' (14)
BIL-*nu-* = *warnu-* 'to burn' (trans.) (2)
BURU$_{14}$ = 'crop(s), harvest' (9) (previously read as EBUR)
DAM-*a-* (comm.) 'wife' (9)
DAM-*atar* (neut.) 'wifehood, marriage' (7)
DI = *ḫanneššar* (neut.) 'legal case' (8)
DIDLI.ḪI.A (plural marker) (used exclusively with Sumerograms) (12) (previously read as AŠ.AŠ.ḪI.A)
DINGIR/DINGIR-*LÌ*/DINGIR-*LÌ-n*(*i*)-, pl. DINGIR.MEŠ = *šiun(i)-* 'god' (1) and (2)
DUMU-(*l*)*a-* (comm.) 'child; son' (1)
DUMU.É.GAL-*i-* (comm.) 'palace official' (plural DUMU.MES.É.GAL)(1)
DUMU.LUGAL-*a-*(plural DUMU.MEŠ LUGAL) (comm.) 'prince' (3)
DUMU.MUNUS-*a-* (comm.) 'daughter' (1) (previously read as DUMU.SAL)
DUMU.NAM.LÚ.U$_{19}$.LU-*(l)a-* = *dandukišnaš* DUMU-*a-* (comm.) 'human being' (6) (previously read as DUMU.NAM.LÚ.ULÙ^{LU})
É = **pēr/parn-* (neut.) 'house' (6)
É.DINGIR-*LÌ* (pl. É.DINGIR.MEŠ) = *šiunaš pēr* (neut.) 'temple' (3)
É.GAL-*LU*$_4$ (neut.) 'palace' (4)
EGIR-*an* = *āppan* 'behind; after' (9)
EGIR-*(ez)zi(ya)-* = *appezzi(ya)-* 'rear-, last' (2)
EGIR-*pa* = *āppa* 'back; again' (3)
EN-*a-* = *išḫā-* (comm.) 'lord, master; owner' (2)
EN.SÍSKUR 'client, patron, sacrificer' (6)
ÉRIN.MEŠ-*t-* (comm.) 'troops' (5) (previously read as ZAB, ERÍN and ERIM)
ÉSAG-*(n)a-* (comm.) 'grain storage pit' (10) (previously read as ARÀḪ)
GAD-*a-* (comm.) '(piece of) cloth' (3)
GAL-*(l)i-* = *šalli-* 'great, large; adult' (2)
GAL LÚ.MEŠ *MEŠEDI* 'chief of the bodyguard'
GAL.DUB.SAR.MEŠ 'chief of the scribes' (10)
GAM = *katta* 'down(ward)' (3) and *kattan* 'below' (7)
GAŠAN 'lady'(5)
GE$_6$-*ant-* = *išpant-* (comm.) 'night' (5) (previously read as MI-*ant-*)
GE$_6$-*i-* = *dankui-* 'dark; black' (2) (previously read as MI-*i-*)
GÉME-*(a/iššar)a-* (comm.) 'servant, slave-(woman)' (11) (previously read as GEME and GEMÉ)
GEŠTIN-*(n)a-* = *wiyana-* (comm.) 'wine' (1)
GI = *nata-* 'reed; arrow' (11)
^{GIŠ}GIDRU-*a-* (comm.) 'staff, stick' (1) (previously read as ^{GIŠ}PA)
GIM-*an* = *māḫḫan* 'when; as; how?' (2, 4)
GÍN 'shekel' (10)
GÍR-*a-* (neut.) 'knife' (1)
GÌR-*a-* (comm.) 'foot' = *pada-* (1)

^{GIŠ}GÌR.GUB-*iš(n)-* = ^{GIŠ}*kuppiš(n)-* 'stool' (§4.89)[251] (1)
GIŠ-*(r)u-* (neut.) 'wood; tree' (1) and (3)
^{GIŠ}GU.ZA 'throne' (13)
GÙB-*(l)a-* 'left-(hand)' (previously read as KAB-*(l)a-*) (4)
GUD-*u-* (comm.) 'bovine, cow, steer' (1) and (7) (also read as GU_4)
GUD.NIGA 'fattened ox' (also read as GU_4.NIGA or GUD.ŠE) (8)
^{LÚ}GUDU$_{12}$-*a-* (comm.) (9) (previously read as ^{LÚ}IM.ME, ^{LÚ}UḪ.ME, or ^{LÚ}GUDÚ) (a kind of priest, ranked below the ^{LÚ}SANGA/^{LÚ}*šankunni*-priests, but above other temple personnel such as exorcists (^{LÚ}AZU/^{LÚ}ḪAL), cooks, table-men, scribes and musicians; Hittite reading most likely *kumra-* comm.; see Hoffner 1996a)
GUL-*aḫḫ-* = *wal(a)ḫ-* 'to strike, hit' (1)
GUNNI-*a-* = *ḫašša-* (comm.) 'hearth' (3)
ḪI.A (plural marker) (used almost exclusively with Sumerograms) (1) (previously read as ḪÁ)
ḪUL-*(p)a-* = *ḫuwappa-* 'bad, evil, malevolent' (2)
ḪUL-*(l)u-* = *idālu-* 'bad, evil; hostile' (3)
ḪUR.SAG-*(r)a-* (comm.) 'mountain' (1)
$^{(UZU)}$Ì (neut.) = *šakan-* (neut.) 'fat; oil' (11) (previously read as ^{UZU}IÀ)
Ì.DÙG.GA 'fine oil' (14) (previously read as IÀ.DUG.GA)
ÍD-*an-* = *ḫapan-* (comm.) 'river' (8)
IGI-*(ez)zi(ya)-* = *ḫantezzi(ya)-* 'front-, foremost; first' (2)
IGI-*wa-* = *šakuwa-* 'eyes' (6)
IKU-*(n)a-* (comm.) (measure of length) (13) (previously read as GAN)
INIM = *uttar* and *memia(n)-* 'word; matter, affair' (6) and (7) (previously read as KA)
ÌR-*(n)a/i-* (comm.) '(male) servant, slave' (1) (also read as ARAD)
ÌR-*(n)aḫḫ-* 'to subject, make one's servant' (13) (also read as ARAD)
ÌR-*(n)ātar* (neut.) 'servitude, bondage, slavery' (14) (also read as ARAD)
^{d}IŠKUR (the Stormgod) (5) (also read ^{d}IM)
ITU-*(m)a-* (comm.) 'month' (= *arma-*) (13)
IZI = *paḫḫur* 'fire' (1) and (6)
KA×U = *aiš* 'mouth' (8)
KASKAL-*(š)a-* = *palša-* (comm.)'path, way; time, instance' (11) (previously read KAS)
KAŠ = *šiyeššar* (neut.) 'beer' (6)
KI = *tēkan* 'earth' (7)
KI.MIN (functions like English 'ditto') (7)
KIR_4 (neut.) 'nose' (11) (previously read as KA×KAK)
KÙ.BABBAR-*i-* (neut.) 'silver' (7) (previously read as KUG.UD)
KUR = *utnē* (neut.) 'land, country' (3) and (9)
^{d}LIŠ '(the goddess) Ishtar' (10)
LÚ-*(n)a/i-* (comm.) 'man, male' (1)

251. The complementation *-iš*, which points to an underlying *kuppiš(n)-*, is found in KBo 20.8 obv. 19 (OS!). Other occurrences of ^{GIŠ}GÌR.GUB may cover the Hittite word *ḫapšalli*.

LÚ ^{GIŠ}BANŠUR (comm.) 'table-man' (server) (9)
LÚ.IGI.NU.GÁL 'blind man' (7)
LÚ.^{GIŠ}TUKUL 'man having a TUKUL obligation' (8) (previously read as LÚ ^{GIŠ}KU)
LÚ.KÚR-*(n)a-* (comm.) 'enemy' (1)
LÚ *ṬĒME* 'messenger' (= Akkad. *amel ṭēme;* the LÚ is not a determinative) (12)
LÚ.U_{19}.LU-*a-* = *antuḫša-* 'person' (comm.) (11) (previously read as LÚ.ULÙ^{LU})
LUGAL-*u-* = *ḫaššu-* (comm.) 'king' (3)
LUGAL-*(u)eznātar* = **ḫaššuweznātar* (neut.) 'kingship' (11)
MA.NA 'mina' (11)
MEŠ (plural marker) (used almost exclusively with Sumerograms) (1)
MU/MU.KAM-*t-* = *wētt-/wītt-* 'year' (§4.95) (5)
^{LÚ}MUḪALDIM-*a-* 'cook' (1) (previously read as ^{LÚ}MU)
MUL = *ḫaštēr-* (comm.) 'star' (see §4.84) (11)
MUNUS-*n-* (comm.) 'woman; wife' (6) (previously read as SAL and MÍ)
MUNUS.LUGAL-*(r)a-* = *ḫaššuššara-* 'queen' (1) (previously read as SAL.LUGAL)
MUNUS.ŠU.GI 'old woman' (medical/ritual practitioner) (8) (previously read as SAL ŠU.GI)
NAM.RA-*a-* = *arnuwala-* (comm.) 'deportee'; i.e., foreign civilian seized by the Hittites and forcibly resettled elsewhere) (11)
NIM.LÀL-*a-* (comm.) 'bee' (14)
NIN-*a-* = *nega-* (comm.) 'sister' (7)
NINDA-*a-* (comm.) 'bread' (1)
NINDA.GUR_4.RA-*i-* (comm.) 'leavened bread, boule' (4) (also read as NINDA.KUR_4.RA)
^{d}NIN.TU-*a-* = ^{d}*Ḫannaḫanna-* (fate goddess) (10)
NU.GÁL '(there) is/are not' (8)
SAG.DU = *ḫaršar* 'head' (also used for 'person') (6)
^{LÚ}SAGI(.A)-*(l)a-* (comm.) 'cupbearer' (7) (previously read as ^{LÚ}QA.ŠU.DU_8(.A) or ^{LÚ}SÌLA.ŠU.DU_8(.A))
^{LÚ}SANGA-*(n)i-* = *šankunni-* (3)
^{LÚ}SIPA-*a-* = *wēštara-* (comm.) 'shepherd' (10) (previously read as ^{LÚ}SIPAD)
SÌR-*RU* = *IZAMMARŪ* = *išḫamiyanzi* 'they sing' (4)
SÍSKUR = *aniur*, *malteššar* or *mukeššar* (neut.) 'sacrifice, ritual' (2, 13) (previously read as ZUR.ZUR or SISKUR.SISKUR). On the variety of Hittite nouns underlying SÍSKUR, see CHD L-N sub *malteššar.*
ŠÀ 'insides; womb' (8), also = **kēr/kard-* 'heart' (9), and = Akkad. *INA* 'in, on, at' (14) (previously read as ŠÀ(G))
ŠAḪ-*a-* (comm.) 'pig' (1)
ŠEŠ-*(n)a-* = *negna-* (comm.) 'brother' (11)
ŠU-*(r)a-* = *keššar(a)-* (comm.) 'hand' (1) and (8)
^{GIŠ}ŠÚ.A-*ki(t)-* 'chair' (13)
TA.ÀM 'time(s)' (with numbers) (14)
TI-*(w)ātar* = *ḫuišwātar* 'life' (6)
$TI_8^{MUŠEN}$ = *ḫāran-* 'eagle' (7) (previously read as Á^{MUŠEN})
TÚG-*a-* (comm.) 'cloth, garment' (2)

TÚG.NÍG.LÁM.MEŠ ‘festive garments’ (10)
TUKU.TUKU-*(at)t-* = *kartimmiyatt-* ‘anger (5)
TUKU.TUKU-*(w)ant-* = *kartimmiyawant-* ‘angry’ (5)
^{GIŠ}TUKUL-*(l)i-* (comm.) ‘weapon’ (11)
TUR ‘small, little’ (9)
^{d}U see ^{d}10
Ú.SAL-*u-* = *wellu-* ‘meadow’ (3)
Ù = *zašḫai-* (noun)/*zašḫiya-* (verb) (12)
UD(.KAM)-*(at)t-* = *šiwatt-* ‘day’ (5) (also read as U_4(.KAM))
^{d}UD.SIG_5 ‘the favorable day’ (as a deity) (8) (also read as U_4.SIG_5)
UDU-*u-* (comm.) ‘sheep’ (6)
UDU.ŠIR-*a/i-* (comm.) ‘ram’ (13)
UGULA ‘chief, head’ (9)
UN-*(š)a-* (comm.) ‘man, human’ (1) (previously read as ÙKU)
UR.GI_7-*(n)a-* (comm.) ‘dog’ (13) (previously read as UR.TÚG or UR.ZÍR)
UR.MAḪ-*a/i-* (comm.) ‘lion’ (1) (= Luwian *walwa/i-*?)
URU-*(ri)ya-* = *ḫappiriya-* ‘city’ (2)
^{d} UTU-*u-* = *Ištanu-* ‘Sun-god’ (4)
^{d}UTU ^{URU}*Arinna* = ‘Sun-goddess of Arinna’ (also written ^{URU}PÚ/TÚL-*na*) (5)
^{d}UTU-*ŠI* ‘my Sungod’ (royal title; usually translated ‘His Majesty’) (4)
^{d}ZA.BA_4.BA_4-*a-* (comm.) (a wargod) (11)
ZÀ.AḪ.LI^{SAR} (neut.) ‘weeds’ (5)
^{LÚ}ZABAR.DAB or ^{LÚ}ZABAR.DIB (comm.) (an official who distributes beverages) (7) (previously read as ^{LÚ}UD.KA.BAR.DIB)
ZAG-*a-* = *irḫa-* (comm.) ‘border (territory)’ (4)
ZAG-*(n)a-* = *kunna-* ‘right-(hand)’ (1)
ZAG.GAR.RA-*(n)a-* = *ištanana-* (comm.) ‘altar, sacrificial table’ (2)
^{UZU}ZAG.LU-*(na)-* = *paltana-* (comm.) ‘shoulder’ (1)
ZI = *ištanza(n)-* ‘soul’ (8)
ZU_9 ‘tooth’ (12) (previously read as KA×UD)
^{d}10 ‘Stormgod’ (2) (also read as ^{d}U)
Akkadian
ABU/ABI ‘father’ (1)
AMMATU ‘ell, yard’ (measure of length) (13)
ANA (marks dative-locative case) (3)
BIBRU ‘rhyton, animal-shaped drinking vessel’ (10)
DINU = *ḫanneššar* (neut.) ‘legal case, dispute’ (4)
ELLU(M) = *arawanni-* ‘free (person)’ (10)
INA ‘in, into’ (marks dative-locative case) (4)
IṢBAT = *ēpta* ‘took, seized’ (12)
^{d}*IŠTAR* ‘(the goddess) Ishtar’ (10, 12)
IŠTU (marks ablative or instrumental case, thus ‘from’ or ‘with’) (4)
-*KA* ‘your’ (sg.) (used only after Sumerograms and Akkadian words) (4)
-*KUNU* ‘your’ (plural)(used only after Sumerograms and Akkadian words) (3)
LIM ‘thousand’ (12)
MÊ = *wātar* ‘water’ (1)

LÚ*MUTU* 'husband' (10)
-*NI* 'our' (used only after Sumerograms and Akkadian words) (4) (12)
NĪŠ DINGIR-*LÌ* 'oath' (4)
NĪŠ DINGIR.MEŠ 'the oaths' (as agents of vengeance) (7)
QADU '(together) with' (9)
QASSU = *keššar(aš)⸗šiš* 'his/her hand' (11)
QATAMMA = *apeniššan* 'thus, so' (2)
d*SÎN-a-* = *arma-* 'moon, Moongod' (9)
ŠA 'of' (marks following logogram as representing a Hittite genitive) (2)
(*ŠA*) *ŠAMÊ* = *nepišaš* 'of heaven' (4)
-*ŠU* 'his' (used only after Sumerograms and Akkadian words) (1)
ŠUM 'name' (= *lāman-*) (2) and (7)
-*ŠUNU* 'their' (used only after Sumerograms and Akkadian words) (4)
ṬĒMU see LÚ *ṬEME* above
ṬUPPU 'clay tablet' (10)
U (written with the sign Ù) 'and, but' (5)
ŪL/UL = *natta* (1)
UŠKĒN = *arkuwāizzi, ḫe(n)kta, ḫinkta, ḫingari* 'bows' (4)
-*YA* 'my' (used only after Sumerograms and Akkadian words) (1)

SOURCES OF EXERCISE SENTENCES MARKED ♦ OR ◊

2.5. Adapted from KBo 11.14 ii 22 (MH/NS).
3.8. KBo 5.6 iii 50–52 NH) with KUR added from dupl. text KBo 14.12 iii 33.
4.4. KBo 20.5 rev.! 10–11 (OH/OS) restored from KBo 22.195 iii! 5–6 (MS).
4.7. Heavily adapted version of KBo 4.3 i 22–24 (NH).
4.9. KBo 5.4 rev. 16–17 (NH).
4.12. KUB 5.1 i 54 (NH).
5.6. Adapted from KUB 30.10 rev. 18 (MH/MS).
5.7. KBo 6.2 i 16–17 (OH/OS) = Laws §10.
5.9. Adapted from KUB 19.18 i 17–18 (NH).
5.13. Adapted from KBo 4.6 obv. 11–14 (NH).
5.14. Adapted from KUB 21.27 iv 13–14 (NH).
5.15. Adapted from KBo 10.2 i 36–37 (OH/NS).
6.2. KBo 5.6 iii 5–6 (NH).
6.3. Adapted from KUB 43.58 i 46–48 (MH/MS).
6.4. KBo 6.2 iv 56–58 (OH/OS), restored from KBo 6.3 iv 55–58 (NS) = Laws §99.
6.5. Adapted from KBo 4.2 i 58–60 (MH/NS).
6.7. KBo 4.8 ii 10–12 (NH).
6.10. Adapted from KBo 20.34 obv. 11 (OH/MS).
6.13. Adapted from KBo 3.1 ii 5–7 (OH/NS).
6.15. KUB 21.27 iv 35–36 (NH).
7.1. Adapted from KUB 14.10 i 6–8 (NH).
7.2. Adapted from HKM 58 5 (MH/MS).
7.3. HKM 58 6–7 (MH/MS).
7.4. KBo 17.1 iii 8–9 (OH/OS).
7.5. KUB 2.10 v 25–26 (OH/NS)
7.6. KUB 19.37 iii 46–48 (NH)
7.7. KUB 30.10 obv. 15 (MH/MS).
7.8. KUB 21.27 ii 5–16 (NH).
7.9. Restored and emended version of KBo 3.1 i 30–31 (OH/NS).
7.10. KUB 14.1 rev. 21–23 (MH/MS).
7.13. KUB 39.7 ii 7–9 (OH/NS).

8.1. KUB 30.21+KUB 39.7 i 2–4 (OH/NS)
8.2. Adapted from KUB 14.8 i 14–15 (NH).
8.3. KBo 17.74 iii 48 (OH/MS), restored from KUB 43.26 iv 7 (OS).
8.6. Restored version of KBo 6.25+KBo 13.35 iii 5–7 (OH/NS).
8.7. KBo 6.2 ii 45 (OH/OS) = Laws §47B.
8.8. KBo 5.8 i 26–27 (NH).
8.9. Adapted from KBo 4.4 iii 36–37 (NH).
8.10. Adapted from KUB 7.60 ii 4–6 (?/NS).
8.11. Adapted from KBo 4.4 iii 43–44 (NH).
8.12. KUB 6.45 iii 13–15 = KUB 6.46 iii 53–54 (NH).
8.13. KUB 26.12 ii 15–16 (NH).
8.14. Adapted from KUB 6.45 iii 23–24 (NH).
8.15. KBo 6.2 ii 14–15 (OH/OS), restored from KBo 6.3 ii 33 (NS) = Laws §38.
9.1. KBo 17.1 i 28–29 (OH/OS).
9.3. KUB 5.6 i 39–41 (NH).
9.4. KBo 17.15 rev. 18 (OH/OS), restored from KBo 17.40 iv 13 (OS).
9.6. KBo 5.13 i 7–9 (NH).
9.7. Restored version of KUB 1.16 ii 53–54 (OH/NS).
9.8. Adapted from KUB 1.16 iii 57–58 (OH/NS).
9.9. Adapted from KBo 5.13 ii 18–20 (NH).
9.10. Adapted from KBo 5.13 ii 20–21 (NH).
9.11. Adapted from KUB 32.117+KUB 35.93 iii 10–11 (OH/OS).
9.12. KUB 8.1 ii 16–17 (NH).
9.13. KUB 2.13 iii 9–11 (OH/NS).
9.14. KBo 15.25 rev. 18 (MH/MS).
9.15. Freely restored version of KBo 5.6 ii 31–33 (NH).
10.1. KBo 5.13 i 15–16 (NH).
10.2. KBo 6.2 i 51–52 (OH/OS) = Laws §23.
10.3. KUB 17.10 i 29–30 (OH/MS).
10.4. KBo 4.2 iii 56–57 (NH), restored from KUB 43.50 obv. 18+KUB 15.36 obv. 10.
10.5. KUB 21.17 iii 9–12 (NH).
10.6. Restored version of KUB 21.17 iii 13–17 (NH).
10.7. KBo 5.6 iv 6–7 (NH).
10.8. Adapted from BrTabl. iv 19–20 (NH).
10.9. Restored version of KBo 26.58 iv 44–46 (Ullik., NS), partly from KUB 36.11 2 and partly from KBo 26.59 iii 32′.
10.10. KBo 6.34 ii 44–45 (MH/NS).
10.11. KBo 6.2 iv 49–50 (OH/OS), restored from KBo 6.3 iv 48–49 (NS) = Laws §96.
10.12. KBo 21.22 obv. 22–25 (OH/MS).
10.13. KBo 2.6 iii 17–18 (NH).
10.14. Adapted from BrTabl. iv 16–20 (NH).
10.15. KBo 15.52 vi 39–45 (pre-NH/NS).
11.4. KUB 29.1 i 19–20 (OH/NS).
11.5. Adapted from KUB 13.2 ii 43–44 (MH/NS).

11.6. BrTabl. ii 43–44 (NH).
11.7. KBo 6.2 i 22–23 (OH/OS), restored from KBo 6.3 i 31–32 (NS) = Laws §12.
11.8. KBo 6.3 i 33 (OH/NS) = Laws §13.
11.9. Restored version of KUB 33.54 ii 13–14 (OH/NS).
11.10. Adapted from KBo 8.35 ii 19–20 (MH/MS).
11.11. Restored version of KBo 17.43 i 10–11 (OH/OS).
11.12. Adapted from KUB 17.21 iv 12–14 (MH/MS).
11.13. KBo 17.4 ii 8–9 (OH/OS),
11.14. KBo 12.42 rev. 6–8 (OH/NS).
11.15. KBo 6.2 iv 12–13 (OH/OS) = Laws §79.
12.1. Adapted from KBo 5.13 i 20–22 (NH).
12.2. KBo 3.4 iii 19–21 (NH).
12.3. KUB 1.1 i 36–38 (Ḫatt., NH).
12.4. Adapted from KUB 1.1 i 40 (Ḫatt., NH).
12.5. Freely restored version of KBo 3.22 obv. 39–42 (OH/OS).
12.6. KBo 4.4 iv 20–21 (NH).
12.7. KBo 6.2 i 9–10 (OH/OS) = Laws §7.
12.8. KBo 3.22 obv. 6–8 (OH/OS).
12.9. KBo 10.2 i 19–21 (OH/NS).
12.10. KBo 5.8 ii 3–5 (NH).
12.11. Restored version of KUB 23.101 ii 19–20 (NH).
12.12. KBo 4.3 i 12 (NH).
12.13. KUB 19.65+KUB 31.13 6–7 (NH) = Ḫatt. iii 46′–47′, restored from KUB 19.64 20–21.
12.14. Adapted from KBo 11.1 obv. 1–2 (NH).
12.15. Restored version of KUB 19.10 i 18–19 (NH) = DŠ 13.
13.2. KUB 12.66 iv 9–10 (OH/NS).
13.3. KUB 31.127+ i 40–49 (OH/NS).
13.4. KUB 33.120 i 8–10 (MH/NS).
13.5. KUB 36.12 i 15 + 33.113 (Ullik., MH/NS).
13.6. KBo 4.4 iv 18–19 (NH).
13.7. Freely restored version of KBo 3.4 i 41–42 (NH).
13.9. KUB 30.15 i 10–11 (NH).
13.10. Adapted from KUB 33.98 iii 15–16 (Ullik., MH/NS).
13.12. Restored version of KUB 30.10 rev. 13–14 (MH/MS).
13.13. KUB 33.106 ii 8–9 (Ullik., MH/NS).
13.14. KUB 9.32 obv. 6–7 (MH/NS).
13.15. KBo 5.6 iii 12–13 (NH).
14.1. KUB 17.10 ii 29–30 (OH/MS).
14.2. KBo 4.4 iii 45–47 (NH).
14.3. KBo 4.4 iii 47–48 (NH).
14.4. KUB 15.34 i 45–46 (MH/MS).
14.5. KBo 5.3 ii 22–23 (MH/NS).
14.7. KBo 4.4 i 41–42 (NH).
14.8. KUB 31.127 i 52–56 (OH/NS).
14.9. KBo 4.14 iii 9 (NH).

14.10. KBo 5.1 i 45–47 (MH/NS).
14.11. KBo 3.1 ii 36–37 (OH/NS).
14.12. KBo 8.35 ii 14–15 (MH/MS).
14.13. Restored and adapted from KBo 16.1 iii 11–14 (NH).
14.15. KUB 43.60 i 10–11 (OH/NS).
14.16. Freely restored version of KBo 4.4 iv 4–5 (NH).
14.17. Restored and excerpted version of KBo 17.75 i 46–47 (OH/NS).